MORMONISM

Zondervan Guide to Cults & Religious Movements

First Series

Unmasking the Cults   *by Alan W. Gomes*
Jehovah's Witnesses   *by Robert M. Bowman, Jr.*
Masonic Lodge   *by George A. Mather and Larry A. Nichols*
Mormonism   *by Kurt Van Gorden*
New Age Movement   *by Ron Rhodes*
Satanism   *by Bob and Gretchen Passantino*
Unification Church   *by J. Isamu Yamamoto*
Mind Sciences   *by Todd Ehrenborg*

Second Series

"Jesus Only" Churches   *by E. Calvin Beisner*
Astrology and Psychic Phenomena   *by André Kole and Terry Holley*
Goddess Worship, Witchcraft and Other Neo-Pagan Movements
    by Craig Hawkins
TM, Hare Krishna and Other Hindu-based Movements
    by Kurt Van Gorden
Dianetics and Scientology   *by Kurt Van Gorden*
Unitarian Universalism   *by Alan W. Gomes*
UFO Cults and Urantia   *by Kenneth Samples and Kevin Lewis*
Buddhism, Taoism and Other Far Eastern Movements
    by J. Isamu Yamamoto

MORMONISM

KURT VAN GORDEN
Author

Alan W. Gomes
Series Editor

ZondervanPublishingHouse
Grand Rapids, Michigan

A Division of HarperCollins*Publishers*

To Dr. Walter R. Martin (1928–1989)

A personal friend, teacher, and mentor who wrote the first Zondervan series on cults (1950s). He taught me to never give up and to contend earnestly for the faith once for all delivered to the saints (Jude 3).

Mormonism
Copyright © 1995 by Kurt Van Gorden

Requests for information should be addressed to:
Zondervan Publishing House
Grand Rapids, Michigan 49530

Library of Congress Cataloging-in-Publication Data

Van Gorden, Kurt.
    Mormonism / Kurt Van Gorden, author.
        p. cm. — (Zondervan guide to cults & religious movements)
    Includes bibliographical references.
    ISBN: 0-310-70401-4 (softcover)
        1. Mormon Church—Controversial literature. 2. Church of Jesus
Christ of Latter-day Saints—Controversial literature. I. Title. II. Series:
Zondervan guide to cults and religious movements.
BX8645.V35   1995
289.3—dc20   94-26654
                                                    CIP

Edited by Patti Picardi
Interior design by Art Jacobs

Printed in the United States of America

95 96 97 98 99 00 /❖ DP/ 10 9 8 7 6 5 4 3 2 1

Contents

89427

 # How to Use This Book

The *Zondervan Guide to Cults and Religious Movements* comprises sixteen volumes, treating many of the most important groups and belief systems confronting the Christian church today. This series distills the most important facts about each and presents a well-reasoned, cogent Christian response. The authors in this series are highly qualified, well-respected professional Christian apologists with considerable expertise on their topics.

For ease of use we have sought to maintain the same "look and feel" for all the books. We designed the structure and layout to help you find the information you need as quickly as possible.

All the volumes are written in outline form. This allows us to pack substantial content into a short book. The major divisions are basically the same from book to book. Each book contains an introduction to the cult, movement, or belief system. The introduction gives a brief history of the group, its organizational structure, and vital statistics such as membership. The theology section is arranged by doctrinal topic, such as God, Christ, sin, and salvation. The movement's position on each topic is set forth objectively, primarily from its own official writings. The group's teachings are then refuted point by point, followed by an affirmative presentation of what the Bible says about the doctrine. Following the theology section is a discussion of witnessing tips. While each witnessing encounter must be handled individually and sensitively, this section provides some helpful general guidelines, including both dos and don'ts. The books also have annotated bibliographies, listing works by the groups themselves as well as books written by Christians in response. Each book concludes with a parallel comparison chart. Arranged topically, the chart juxtaposes direct quotations from the cultic literature in the left column with the biblical refutation on the right.

One potential problem with a detailed outline is that it is easy to lose one's place in the overall structure. To overcome this problem we have provided graphical "signposts" at the top of the odd-numbered pages. Functioning like a "you are here" map in a shopping mall, these graphics show your place in the outline, including the sections that come before and after your current position. In the theology section we have also used "icons" in the margins to make clear at a glance whether the material is being presented from the cultic or Christian viewpoint. For example, in the Mormonism volume those portions of the outline presenting the Mormon position are indicated with a picture of the angel Moroni in the margin. The biblical view is shown by a drawing of a Bible.

We hope you will find these books useful as you seek "to give an answer to everyone who asks you to give the reason for the hope that you have" (1 Peter 3:15).

—Alan W. Gomes, Ph.D.
Series Editor

Part I: Introduction

I.Historical Background

A. Joseph Smith, Jr. (1805–44): Founder

   1. Smith's Family Background (1805–20)

      a. Smith was born to Joseph and Lucy Smith on December 23, 1805, in Sharon, Vermont.

      b. Smith was the fourth child of nine who survived.

      c. In 1817, the Smith family settled on a farm in Palmyra, New York.

      d. Smith's parents were inactive Protestants.

         (1) Joseph and Lucy Smith blended superstitious folklore[1] and occult dabbling[2] into the home life.[3]

         (2) His mother, two brothers, and a sister later joined the Presbyterian Church in Palmyra, New York.

   2. Early Religious Visions and Experiences (1820–27)

      a. Vision of the Father and Jesus Christ (1820).[4]

---

[1]*The Encyclopedia of Mormonism* (Daniel H. Ludlow, ed., 5 vols. [New York: Macmillan, 1992]) is a fresh and honest attempt by scholarly Mormons to openly discuss controversial Mormon history and beliefs. It admits that Joseph Smith, Jr., and his father were hired to dig for buried treasure (3:1348).

[2]D. Michael Quinn, former Professor of American History at Brigham Young University, wrote a revealing exposé on the Smith family's occultism in *Early Mormonism and the Magic World View* (Salt Lake City: Signature Books, 1987). Quinn painstakingly documents his work and reproduces photographs of Joseph Smith's seer stones, magic dagger, talisman, and other occult paraphernalia. See also Jerald Tanner and Sandra Tanner, *Mormonism, Magic, and Masonry* (Salt Lake City: Utah Lighthouse Ministry, 1983).

[3]That Joseph Smith, Jr., was personally involved in the occult is indisputable. In 1971 Rev. Wesley P. Walters discovered the original court bill showing Smith's arrest, conviction, and fine for "glass-looking" the practice of finding lost items or buried treasure by looking at a stone called a seer stone. The court bill has been reproduced by a number of writers (e.g., Walter Martin, *The Maze of Mormonism* [Santa Ana: Vision House Publishers, 1978]; Jerald Tanner and Sandra Tanner, *The Changing World of Mormonism* [Chicago: Moody Press, 1980]; and Wesley P. Walters, *Joseph Smith's Bainbridge, N.Y., Court Trials* [Salt Lake City: Modern Microfilm Co., n.d.]).

[4]The official version was written by Smith in 1843 (*Times and Seasons*, 6 vols. [Nauvoo, Ill.: The Church of Jesus Christ of Latter-day Saints], 3:728). In 1851 it was added to the Mormon scriptures, Pearl of Great Price (Salt Lake City: The Church of Jesus Christ of Latter-day Saints, 1982, Joseph Smith 1:5–20). There are nine conflicting versions of the First Vision that give contradictory details on such issues as Smith's age at the time of the vision (14–16), who appeared (Son alone, Father and Son, Son with angels, angels alone), how they appeared (one at a time, together), and who spoke (Father, Son, or angels). The first account, written in 1831, greatly differs from the 1843 account noted above. See Jerald Tanner and Sandra Tanner, *Mormonism—Shadow or Reality?*, 5th ed. (Salt Lake City: Utah Lighthouse Ministry, 1987), 143–62.

(1) In the Spring of 1820, when Smith was fourteen years old, he claimed that a revival broke out in the Presbyterian, Baptist, and Methodist churches of Palmyra.[5]

(2) Smith was not willing to join in the excitement, but questioned which, if any, church was true.

(3) After reading James 1:5, which says that God will give wisdom to those who ask, Smith claimed that he went to the woods to pray and there received a vision of God the Father and Jesus Christ.

(4) When Smith asked them which church to join, he was told, "Join none of them, for they were all wrong," and that "all their creeds were an abomination in his sight; that those professors were all corrupt."[6]

b. Moroni and the Golden Plates (1823–27)

(1) Smith claimed that an angel named Moroni appeared to him on September 21, 1823.

(2) Moroni said he was a former inhabitant of America who, shortly before his death, buried some golden plates which recorded the history of his people and the fullness of the gospel.

(3) Moroni said Smith would translate the "Reformed Egyptian hieroglyphics"[7] on these golden plates, using special stones called the Urim and Thummim[8] (The Book of Mormon is Smith's alleged translation of the golden plates although he knew no language other than English).

(4) The following day, as Smith was working in a field, Moroni appeared to him again and took him to a hill called Cumorah, where he showed Smith the golden plates and the Urim and Thummim. Moroni forbade Smith to remove the plates, due

---

[5]According to the church records for all three denominations in Palmyra, there was no widespread revival affecting all three churches until the fall of 1824. The research of Rev. Wesley P. Walters shows that the records of 1819–23 are devoid of revivals—some churches even lost membership (*New Light On Mormon Origins From the Palmyra* (N.Y.) *Revival* [La Mesa, Calif.: Utah Christian Tract Society, 1967]). Mormon historians James B. Allen and Leonard J. Arrington wrote, "What evidence do we have, other than the word of Joseph Smith, that there was 'an unusual excitement on the subject of religion' in the vicinity of Palmyra in 1820? Up to this point little such evidence has been uncovered, and Walters challenged the story ..." (*Brigham Young University Studies* [Provo: Brigham Young University, Spring 1969], 272).

[6]Pearl of Great Price, Joseph Smith 1:19.

[7]The nonexistence of the Reformed Egyptian hieroglyphics is a problem for Mormon scholars. Yet they lack any evidence that the Reformed Egyptian ever even existed outside of the mind of Joseph Smith.

[8]The Urim and Thummim, translated "lights and perfections," are mentioned in the Old Testament as two stones set in Aaron's breastplate (Ex. 28:30). They sometimes were used by the high priest to determine God's will (Num. 27:21); see *Encyclopedia of the Bible*, ed. Walter A. Elwell (Grand Rapids: Baker, 1988), 2:2117. For Joseph Smith, however, they somehow appeared in America with the golden plates of the Book of Mormon. They are described as two stones set in silver bows, much like spectacles. Joseph Smith would look into these stones to translate the Book of Mormon; see Ludlow, *Encyclopedia of Mormonism*, 4:1498.

to his age (seventeen), and commanded him to return to that same place annually for four years.

(5) On September 22, 1827, Moroni gave Smith permission to dig up the golden plates, along with the Urim and Thummim, and to begin to translate them.

3. Attempts to Authenticate the Book of Mormon[9]

  a. Dr. Charles Anthon

    (1) Martin Harris, Smith's neighbor, was to sell his farm to subsidize the cost of printing the Book of Mormon.

    (2) Smith copied some of the Reformed Egyptian characters on a piece of paper for Mr. Harris, who then took the paper to Dr. Charles Anthon, the esteemed linguist and professor at Columbia College in New York.

    (3) According to Joseph Smith, Dr. Anthon confirmed the authenticity of the characters and translation until Mr. Harris told him that they came from an angel, whereupon Anthon destroyed his certification.[10]

    (4) Anthon later wrote a testimony that contradicts Smith's account, saying that Harris did indeed present him with the transcription, but that Anthon declared the characters to be perfectly nonsensical and anything but "Egyptian hieroglyphics."[11]

  b. "Witnesses" to the Plates

    (1) Oliver Cowdery, David Whitmer, and Martin Harris claimed that, while in the company of Smith (June 1829), the angel Moroni appeared to them and was holding the golden plates.[12]

---

[9]Recent attempts to authenticate the Book of Mormon through archaeology have failed miserably. Most notable is the work of Thomas Steward Ferguson, founder of the Archaeology Department at Brigham Young University. His revealing manuscript at the close of his career shows that no coins, cities, people, plants, animals, or languages of the Book of Mormon have ever been discovered. See *Ferguson's Manuscript Unveiled* (Salt Lake City: Utah Lighthouse Ministry, 1988).

[10]Pearl of Great Price, Joseph Smith–History 1:63–65, says that Dr. Anthon recognized the characters as "Egyptian, Chaldaic, Assyriac and Arabic."

[11]In a letter dated on February 17, 1834, Professor Anthon called Martin Harris's account "perfectly false," claiming it "was all a trick, perhaps a hoax" (E. D. Howe, *Mormonism Unveiled* [Painsville, Ohio: E. D. Howe, 1834]). Anthon's letter is reproduced in Martin, *The Kingdom of the Cults*, rev. ed. (Minneapolis: Bethany House, 1985), 181–82.

[12]These testimonies are not without conflict. David Whitmer admitted before his death that they beheld "the vision of the angel," not a physical manifestation (Whitmer, *An Address To All Believers In Christ*, 1887, 32). Harris claimed, "I never saw the gold plates, only in a visionary or entranced state" (as quoted by Francis W. Kirkham in *A New Witness For Christ in America*, 2 vols. [Salt Lake City: Utah Printing, 1959], 2:348). An official Mormon publication also contained a poem in 1848 stating that Oliver Cowdery had denied his testimony of the Book of Mormon (*Times and Seasons*, 2:482).

(2) Shortly afterward, eight others allegedly received a special manifestation of the angel and the plates while accompanied by Smith.[13]

4. The Priesthood Conferred (1829)

   a. The Aaronic Priesthood

   (1) Joseph Smith claimed to restore Christianity to the earth.

   (2) One of Smith's first acts of restoration was to reinstate the authoratative priesthood. In May 1829, while he and Oliver Cowdery were praying in a forest near Bainbridge, Pennsylvania, John the Baptist allegedly appeared to them and conferred the Aaronic priesthood upon them.[14]

   (3) Mormons claim that the Aaronic priesthood gives them the authority to baptize and assist in sacramental service.

   b. The Melchizedek Priesthood

   (1) Again in May 1829, Oliver Cowdery and Joseph Smith were praying in the woods when, they claimed, Peter, James, and John appeared to them and conferred the Melchizedekian priesthood upon them.[15]

   (2) Mormons claim that the Melchizedekian priesthood gives them the authority to govern the church and to practice the "laying on of hands" to impart the "gift of the Holy Ghost."[16]

5. Translation and Publication of the Book of Mormon (1830)

   a. Joseph Smith translated the Book of Mormon with the aid of his seer stone.[17] The Urim and Thummin were not used; he instead used an egg-shaped, chocolate-covered seer stone.

   b. Smith reportedly sat behind a curtain and read the translated text to various scribes, including his wife, Emma, and Book of Mormon witnesses, Martin Harris and Oliver Cowdery.

   c. The Book of Mormon was published in March 1830.

---

[13]Upon Joseph Smith's death in 1844, all eight witnesses left Mormonism to follow James Strang. Like Smith before him, Strang claimed to find buried plates and translate them. Later the witnesses split company and followed other splinter groups, such as William E. McLellin, the Shakers, and the Reorganized Latter-day Saints movement under Emma Smith, the wife of Joseph Smith.

[14]Biblically, the Aaronic priesthood could only be held by a descendant of Levi (Ex. 4:14; 28:1), hence the Levitical priesthood. Its purpose was to offer sacrifices for Israel (Heb. 5:1–3). There is no need for the Aaronic or Levitical priesthood after Jesus' crucifixion, since Jesus is the ultimate sacrifice for sins (Heb. 7:27; 9:11–14).

[15]There are only two people in the Bible who had the Melchizedekian priesthood: Melchizedek and Jesus (Heb. 7:11–17). Jesus continues forever in this role and has an unchangeable priesthood (Heb. 7:24). Concerning the priesthood of all true Christians, see 1 Peter 2:5–9.

[16] See Doctrine and Covenants 49:14 and Articles of Faith 4.

[17]Some Mormon historians now publish this fact; see James B. Allen and Glen M. Leonard, *The Story of the LatterSaints*, rev. ed. (Salt Lake City: Deseret Book Co., 1992), 41. See also Deseret News, Church News section, 20 September 1969, 16.

6. The Mormon Church (1830)

   a. Smith officially founded the Mormon Church as The Church of Christ on April 6, 1830, in Fayette, New York.

   b. After two name changes they settled on the Church of Jesus Christ of Latter-day Saints in 1834.

7. Smith's "Translation" of the Bible (1831)[18]

   a. Joseph Smith began to "translate" the King James Version of the Bible in 1831, without referring to Hebrew or Greek manuscripts.

   b. Smith claimed that he used "the gift and power of God" to translate the Bible. In other words, his "translation" was based on supposed direct revelation.

8. Continuing Revelations (1833–44)

   a. Smith continued to receive revelations and published them as The Book of Commandments in 1833.

   b. This was enlarged and later published as the Doctrine and Covenants in 1835. Additional revelations were added through the years.[19]

   c. Some of Smith's revelations were gathered post-mortem and published as The Pearl of Great Price (1851).

9. Smith's "Martyrdom" (1844)

   a. Joseph Smith had established several strongholds for early Mormonism, including Kirtland, Ohio, Independence, Missouri, and Nauvoo, Illinois.

   b. Joseph Smith (who was mayor of Nauvoo), Smith's brother Hyrum, and fourteen Mormon leaders were being held in Carthage, Illinois, on charges of rioting, after ordering an opposing newspaper office destroyed.

      (1) They ordered the destruction to retaliate against the paper for its criticism of the Mormons.

      (2) An additional charge of treason was leveled against the men.

   c. An angry mob stormed the jail where Joseph and Hyrum Smith were being held.

   d. The Smiths were armed with a smuggled six-shooter and single-shot pistol, but were outgunned by the mob.

   e. Joseph and Hyrum Smith died in the gun battle on June 27, 1844.[20]

---

[18]The Joseph Smith Translation is not a translation in the truest sense of the word, since it is not from one language to another. Mormons believe, however, that a translation took place by the power of God, without Smith seeing any manuscripts in the original languages.

[19]The standard abbreviation for the Doctrine and Covenants is D & C in Mormon writings.

[20]Mormons refer to Joseph Smith as a martyr. He did not die a martyr without a fight; he shot three men in the mob, two of whom later died (*Documentary History of the Church*, 7 vols. [Salt Lake City: Deseret Book Co., 1976], 7:102).

B. *Brigham Young (1801–77): Successor to Joseph Smith*
   1. Young's Achievements
      a. Young was known as a powerful leader who held the Mormons together amidst much hardship.
      b. Young held equal esteem as Smith in the eyes of Mormons.
      c. Mormons esteem Young as a prophet, frontiersman, pioneer, colonizer (directing the establishment of 400 colonies), Indian liaison, business entrepreneur, industrialist, territorial governor, and arts enthusiast.
         (1) He founded Brigham Young Academy (now BYU).
         (2) He was husband of 53 wives and father to 57 children.
   2. The Move to Utah
      a. In August 1844, Young officially replaced Smith as prophet.
      b. Young began making plans to follow the Oregon Trail and to move the 12,000 Latter-day Saints westward.
      c. Young, along with a select band of pioneers, arrived at the Great Salt Lake Valley in July 1847.
         (1) The Mormons virtually carved an empire out of this barren land.
         (2) The California gold rush and the opening of the transcontinental railroad greatly increased the value of their property.
      d. Brigham Young ruled over the Utah Territory until his death in 1877.

C. *Succession of Prophets After Brigham Young (1877–Present)*
   1. There have been fourteen prophets of the Mormon Church since its beginning. The fifteenth was to be named in March 1995.
   2. The prophet usually enters his office after serving as the head of the quorum of the twelve Mormon apostles.[21]
   3. Some of the noteworthy accomplishments of successive prophets are:
      a. *Wilford Woodruff* (1807–98)
         (1) Woodruff was the fourth prophet of the Mormon Church (1887–98).
         (2) Woodruff banned plural marriage and saw the Utah Territory become a state in 1896.
      b. *Joseph F. Smith* (1838–1918)
         (1) Smith was the sixth prophet of the Mormon Church (1901–18).
         (2) Even though he was convicted of polygamy in 1906, Smith is responsible for improving the image of the Mormon Church in America.

---

[21]Concerning Mormon apostles, see section III.B.2 below.

    (3) Smith was the first to formalize Mormon theology, later published as *Gospel Doctrine.*

  c. *Joseph Fielding Smith* (1876–1972)[22]

    (1) Smith was the tenth prophet of the Mormon Church (1970–72).

    (2) Smith is the first prophet to be classified as a theologian by Latter-day Saints.

    (3) He finished most of his writings while he was an apostle, but during his presidency he reaffirmed their content as authoritative: "What I have taught in the past, I would teach and write again."[23]

  d. *Spencer W. Kimball* (1895–1985)

    (1) Kimball was the twelfth prophet of the Mormon Church (1973–85).

    (2) Kimball renovated Mormon Church government and had all four Mormon scriptures revised.

    (3) He opened sixteen temples and had eleven others in the making.

    (4) Kimball offered the priesthood to formerly banned races, particularly blacks and American Indians.[24]

    (5) Kimball doubled the missionary efforts and brought over 2,250,000 new members into the church.

  e. *Ezra Taft Benson* (1899–1994)

    (1) Benson was the thirteenth prophet of the Mormon Church (1985 – 1994).

    (2) Benson's contribution was his emphasis on the Book of Mormon: he launched a campaign for its worldwide distribution.

  f. *Howard W. Hunter* (1907–1995)

    (1) Hunter became the fourteenth prophet of the Mormon Church (1994) and died just nine months later in March 1995.

    (2) Hunter, a former corporate attorney, was the first Mormon prophet born in the twentieth century.

D. *Turning Points in Mormon History*

  1. Early Growth of Mormonism Under Sidney Rigdon and Parley Pratt

---

[22]There were two Mormon prophets named Joseph Fielding Smith. They are distinguished by the form of their middle name. The sixth prophet is designated as Joseph F. Smith, who was the father of the tenth prophet, designated as Joseph Fielding Smith. These are not to be confused with the first Mormon prophet, Joseph Smith, Jr. When the name Joseph Smith is used with no other designation, it refers to Joseph Smith, Jr.

[23]From the October *Conference Report* (Salt Lake City: Church of Jesus Christ of Latter-day Saints, 1970), 5.

[24]See the discussion on racism in section I.D.7 below.

a. Kirtland, Ohio, had an established work of the Disciples of Christ movement, with Sidney Ridgon and Parley Pratt as preachers.

b. Pratt converted to Mormonism in 1830 while visiting Newark, New York, and returned to Ohio and preached Mormonism among his friends.

c. Rigdon's church members were baptized into Mormonism (130 over a period of a few months) with no apparent protest by Rigdon, who was baptized a Mormon in December of 1830.

d. Some skeptical Disciples protested that Rigdon was aligned with Smith all along, and recalled how many of Rigdon's sermons laid the groundwork for the large conversion to Mormonism.

e. This sudden growth made Mormonism a visible entity.

2. The Mormon War (1838)

a. The so-called Mormon War took place in Missouri.

b. Mobs in Missouri had harassed Mormon settlers.

(1) On July 4, 1838, Sidney Rigdon delivered the "Salt Sermon" to Mormons, taken from Matthew 5:13.

(2) Rigdon called for a "war of extermination" against any harassing mobs "till the last drop of their blood is spilled."[25]

c. The Mormons formed a band of "destroying angels" called the Danites, whose job was to seek revenge; fights and a gun battle broke out in August and October with men killed on both sides.

d. This explosive situation consummated in a massacre-style attack by 200 troops upon 30 Mormons at the home of Jacob Haun. Seventeen Mormons were killed, including one child.

3. Joseph Smith's Political Activities

a. Joseph Smith entered the political arena and served as mayor of Nauvoo, Illinois, which had become the largest city on the Mississippi River.

b. He eventually organized a militia, heading it as General Joseph Smith.

c. In 1844 Smith made his bid to run for President of the United States, with Sidney Rigdon as his running mate.

d. Smith's political movement met with opposition, and resulted in his death.[26]

4. The Utah War (1857)

a. This war became a standoff between President James Buchanan and Utah Territorial Governor Brigham Young. Buchanan insisted upon appointing "Gentile" judges and officials to wrestle the Utah Territory away from Mormon leaders.

---

[25]Allen and Leonard, *Story of the Latter-day Saints*, 133.

[26]See section I.A.9 above.

    b. President Buchanan sent an army battalion to Utah to reestablish order after Mormons had run out "Gentile" officials.

    c. Although no shots were fired, several hundred U.S. army troops died of hardships caused by Mormons who plundered their cattle and food stock, leaving them without supplies during a severe winter.

5. Mountain Meadows Massacre (1857)

    a. The Mountain Meadows Massacre was a tragic slaughter perpetrated by the Mormons, just north of St. George, Utah.

    b. A wagon train of 120 people from Arkansas who were bound for California were killed by Indians and Mormons disguised as Indians.

      (1) Mormon leaders planned the attack as revenge for years of persecution in Illinois and Missouri.

      (2) Mormon leaders dressed as Indians to make the massacre appear to be a random Indian attack on a wagon train.

    c. In his trial, conviction, and execution, John D. Lee, a member of the Mormon Council of fifty, became the criminal scapegoat for other Mormon leaders.[27]

6. Polygamy (1842–90)

    a. Polygamy was the offense that prevented Utah from becoming a state until 1896.

    b. About 15 to 20 percent of Mormons practiced polygamy, believing it to be sanctioned by divine revelation.

    c. Joseph Smith had 27 wives and Brigham Young married 53 women.

    d. Congressional anti-polygamy laws and harsh opposition by women's groups in the late 1800s led to the new "revelation" by prophet Wilford Woodruff in 1890 that plural marriage would no longer be practiced.

7. Racism (1830–1978)

    a. The divine "curse" placed on Negroes and American Indians is outlined in two Mormon scriptures.

      (1) The Book of Mormon says the American Indians' sins caused them to become "dark and loathsome" (1 Nephi 12:23) as opposed to "white, and exceedingly fair and delightsome" (2 Nephi 5:21).

      (2) The Book of Moses, in the Pearl of Great Price, says that "blackness" came upon the sons of Canaan (Moses 7:8), who Mormons identify as Negroes.

---

[27]John Doyle Lee wrote a manuscript (published post-mortem as *Mormonism Unveiled; or the Life and Confessions of the Mormon Bishop, John D. Lee* [St. Louis: Ryan, Rand and Co., 1877]), in which he confesses his crime and charges the Mormon Church with making him the scapegoat. Juanita Brooks, a Mormon historian, wrote the definitive work on this subject, *The Mountain Meadows Massacre* (Stanford: Stanford University Press, 1950).

b. The divine curse disqualified blacks and Indians from receiving the Mormon priesthood.

c. This teaching was protested as racist at various times, most intensely in the 1960s and '70s by those in the civil rights movement.

d. Mormon prophet Spencer W. Kimball received a new "revelation" on June 9, 1978, releasing the racist ban; thus, American Indians and blacks were allowed to attain the Mormon priesthood.

II. Vital Statistics and Activities

A. Membership Figures

1. Total world membership is 9 million.

2. The membership in the United States is 4.5 million.

3. Their growth rate ranges between 250,000 and 300,000 new baptisms annually; 75.3 percent of these claim a previous Christian affiliation.[28]

B. Missionary Activities

1. The Mormon missionary program requires teenagers to volunteer two years of service. Over 40,000 missionaries serve in 200 missions around the world.

2. Each missionary baptizes about six people a year.

3. House-to-house tracking and proselytizing those within Christian denominations is their major thrust.

C. Literature Distribution

1. A multimillion-dollar advertising budget nets the Mormons an annual distribution of over three million copies of the Book of Mormon.

2. The two main sources for promoting the Book of Mormon are major periodicals and television commercials.

3. Occasionally, the Mormon Church will offer a free family video through a television commercial.

4. An assortment of brochures is distributed through the visitor centers adjacent to Mormon temples.

D. Church Wealth

1. The Mormon Church reportedly brings in three million dollars daily in tithes alone (see F.1 below).

2. The financial prudence of the Mormon hierarchy has made it a wealthy organization; with business and land holdings totaling over ten billion dollars, it is second only to the Catholic Church in wealth.

---

[28]*Eternity Magazine*, July 1978, 9.

E. *Mormon Temples*

1. The Mormons build elaborate temples worldwide. Currently there are fifty with an additional dozen in the planning stages.

2. Three important functions are performed in Mormon temples:

   a. temple endowment ceremonies[29]

   b. eternal marriages[30]

   c. baptism for the dead[31]

3. One can only enter a temple with a "temple recommend" card, obtainable after a stringent interview on moral conduct by one's Bishop.

4. Special garments are worn by Mormons day and night.

   a. Special temple garments are worn under regular street clothing by temple-worthy Mormons as a reminder of his endowments.

   b. These two-piece, light-weight undergarments have special markings on the breast, navel, and knee which relate to rituals within the temple.

5. Some of the symbolism and ceremony practiced in the Mormon temple is derived from the Freemasons, with whom Joseph Smith had been affiliated.[32]

F. *Practices, Customs, and Values*

1. Tithing

   a. Mormons are asked to tithe one-tenth of their income (D & C 119:4).

   b. No offering plate is passed; the local Bishop is responsible for collecting the tithe.

2. Restrictions on Food, Drink, Etc.

   a. Joseph Smith gave a "Word of Wisdom" revelation (D & C 89) that forbade all hot drinks, tobacco (except for treating bruises and sick cattle), and alcohol (except for washing the body), and taught

---

[29]Worthy Mormons particpate in temple rituals and are instructed in ordinances and covenants to guarantee entrance to the highest level of heaven. Once the endowments are completed, worthy Mormons may stand proxy for endowments conferred upon the dead.

[30]Eternal marriage to a Mormon is for time and eternity. They believe that a faithful man will call his wife from the grave for exaltation in a celestial kingdom.

[31]Living worthy Mormons may be baptized by proxy on behalf of the dead by taking the name of the deceased upon themselves during water baptism. See the refutation in Part II, section VIII.C.3.

[32]Mormon writers are typically silent when it comes to connections between Freemasonry and Mormon temple rituals. The connection, however, between Freemasonry and Mormonism is beyond dispute; the question remaining is the depth of the relationship. Mormon historians Allen and Leonard gave barely more than passing notice in their revised edition of *The Story of the Latter-day Saints* (1992, 174–75), and failed to mention Joseph Smith's and Brigham Young's Masonic membership. Dean C. Jessee edited Joseph Smith's personal journals, wherein, under the March 15, 1842 entry, we find that Smith "officiated as grand chaplain at the Installation of the Nauvoo Lodge of Free Masons" (*The Papers of Joseph Smith*, 2 vols. [Salt Lake City: Deseret Book Co., 1992], 2:370).

For a thorough study of the Masonic connection to Mormon temple rituals from a Christian perspective, see Jerald Tanner and Sandra Tanner, *Evolution of the Mormon Temple Ceremony, 1842–1990* (Salt Lake City: Utah Lighthouse Ministry, 1990); idem, *Mormonism, Magic, and Masonry*.

that meat should be consumed sparingly (e.g., only in cold winter months or famine).

b. The Word of Wisdom mentions nothing about caffeine, even though coffee and tea are rejected upon that basis. Strangely, hot chocolate (a caffeinated beverage) is permitted by Mormon leaders.

3. Family Lifestyle

a. Non-Mormons normally regard Mormons as hard-working, morally strict, law-abiding citizens.

b. Mormons promote large families, either natural or adopted.

c. Mormon Church advertisements portray a paradisiacal family. However, the state of Utah, which is the largest sampling of Mormonism's social influence (being 80 percent Mormon), is equal or worse than the national average on many important family-related moral issues.[33]

d. Devout Mormons hold "Family Home Evening" every Monday evening, where families are encouraged to participate in activities such as games and crafts.

4. Education

a. Utah has a lower high school drop-out rate than the national statistics.

b. Mormons often build Mormon Seminaries and Institutes of Religion next to high schools and colleges, both for proselytizing and for educating young Mormons.

c. Brigham Young University boasts 30,000 students on two campuses.

G. Related Groups

There have been over 125 factions of the Mormon Church since the days of Joseph Smith. Most hold to at least the Bible and the Book of Mormon, while others observe parts of Smith's additional revelations.

1. The Reorganized Church of Jesus Christ of Latter-day Saints

a. This is the largest existing splinter group with 240,000 people.

b. It began in 1860 under the direction of Joseph Smith's eldest son, Joseph Smith III.

c. They were called the "Josephites" because of their rejection of the "Brighamites'" teachings on polytheism, "Adam-god," polygamy, and blood atonement.[34]

---

[33]Divorce, street gangs, prostitution (since the 1890s), teenage suicide, teenage pregnancy, and illegitimate births are notable social problems in Utah, ranking high in national averages. See *Utah Holiday Magazine*, June 1980, 35; and *The Denver Post*, 21 November 1982, EM–30; *Rocky Mountain Magazine*, January 1980, 25.

[34]The terms "Josephites" and "Brighamites" were commonly used through the 1930s but now are antiquated. These doctrines are discussed in Part II, sections II.B.2 (polytheism); VII.B.3 (Adam-god); V.B.3 (polygamy); and VIII.B.4.f (blood atonement).

d. They accept the Bible, the Book of Mormon (1837 version), and only portions of the Doctrine and Covenants.

e. They reject the Pearl of Great Price, plurality of gods, the teaching that God is a man, the "Mother God" doctrine,[35] celestial marriage, baptism for the dead, and genealogy work.

2. Fundamentalist Mormons

a. The other major factions are the fundamentalist Mormons, or polygamist clans.

b. They rejected the 1890 revelation of Wilford Woodruff and opted to continue practicing polygamy to this day.[36]

c. There are currently up to 30,000 practicing Mormon polygamist families in the western United States.

III. Church Structure and Government

A. *Church Structure*

1. Branches

a. A Branch is a local congregation of Mormons.

b. Branches usually number fewer than 200 members.

c. The head of a Branch is a Branch President.

2. Wards

a. A Ward is a local congregation of 200 to 800 members.

b. Wards are determined by geographical divisions; when it grows too large it is subdivided into two new Wards.

c. Wards are headed by a Bishop.

3. Stakes

a. A Stake center is a collection of five to twelve Wards in an area.

b. Stakes usually share the same worship building by operating on different schedules.

c. Stakes may include the Wards within one city or the Wards and Branches spanning hundreds of square miles, depending upon the density of population.

d. The Stake President is responsible to the church authorities in Salt Lake City and administers the church policies to the Wards under him.

4. Areas

a. An Area is a large geographical district taking in Stakes, Wards, and Branches.

---

[35] Although these doctrines were taught by Smith, the RLDS Church rejects them. The "Mother God" doctrine is discussed in Part II, section II.A.4 below.

[36] See Steven J. Shields, *Divergent Paths of the Restoration* (Bountiful, Utah: Restoration Research, 1984), where Shields documents 125 splinter groups of Mormonism, many of which practice polygamy.

      b. An area is supervised by three authorities from the Quorums of the Seventy (see B.3 below).

  5. Headquarters

      a. The Mormon Church headquarters is in Salt Lake City, Utah.

      b. The Church administers its affairs internationally from a twenty-six-story building.

B. Church Government

  1. First Presidency

      a. The Prophet holds the highest rank in church government.

      b. The Prophet and two counselors form the First Presidency.

      c. They are considered living oracles of God.

  2. Council of the Twelve Apostles

      a. The Council of the Twelve Apostles is directly under the First Presidency.

      b. The head of the Quorum of the Twelve usually becomes the next prophet.

  3. The First and Second Quorums of the Seventy

      a. The Quorums of the Seventy assist in church government affairs and are traveling representatives of the church.

      b. Each is assigned a geographical area of the world over which he presides.

      c. There was one Quorum of the Seventy until 1989, when the Second Quorum of the Seventy was added by church officials because of growth in membership.

      d. Seven men are chosen from the first quorum to preside over both groups (called the First Council of the Seventy).

  4. The Presiding Bishopric

      a. This line of authority consists of three men who preside over the bishops worldwide.

      b. Their duties consist of the temporal affairs of the church, such as collection of the tithes from stakes, distribution of funds for the poor, and the design of stake centers.

  5. The General Authorities[37]

      a. The General Authorities of the Mormon Church consist of all of the above mentioned groups.

---

[37]Mormons pride themselves on "unpaid clergy." BYU President Rex Lee points out, "There is no such thing as a professional Mormon cleric. . . ." He adds, "Even the ministers of local congregations and larger units, like bishops, state presidents, and regional representatives, are unpaid ministers" (*What Do Mormons Believe?*) [Salt Lake City: Deseret Book Co., 1992], 74). The claim for unpaid clergy is disputed in Lee Tom Perry's article, where he said, "They [general authorities] receive modest living allowances" (Ludlow, *Encyclopedia of Mormonism*, 3:1045). The modest living allowance was revealed by Seventies member Paul H. Dunn in 1983 as $40,000 (*Wall Street Journal*, 9 November 1983, 1). This was 327 percent above the average income of $12,216.83 in 1983.

b. General Authorities are the only representatives who can act officially in the name of the church.

c. Their decisions on doctrinal matters are considered binding until further change.

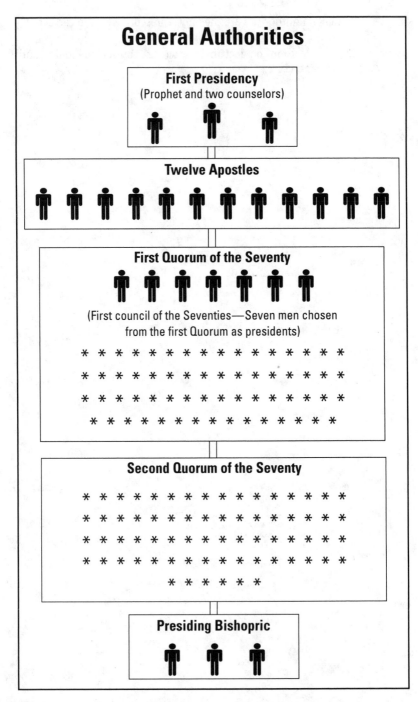

General Authorities

First Presidency
(Prophet and two counselors)

Twelve Apostles

First Quorum of the Seventy

(First council of the Seventies—Seven men chosen
from the first Quorum as presidents)

Second Quorum of the Seventy

Presiding Bishopric

Part II:
Theology

I. Sources of Authority

A. *The Mormon View of Authority and Scripture Briefly Stated*

  1. Standard Works

    a. The Bible

      (1) Mormons prefer the King James Version.

      (2) The Joseph Smith Translation was added to the footnotes of the King James Version in the 1983 edition published by the Mormon Church (see Part I, section 1.A.7).[38]

    b. The Book of Mormon[39]

      (1) The original 1830 edition has undergone several revisions.[40]

      (2) The current text is the revised 1981 edition.

    c. Doctrine and Covenants[41]

      (1) This work was originally published as the Book of Commandments in 1833.[42]

      (2) The current edition contains the text from 1920 with the revised section headings from 1982.

    d. Pearl of Great Price[43]

      (1) This book was originally published in 1851.

      (2) The current edition (1982) contains slight textual changes from the original.[44]

---

[38]Some portions of the Joseph Smith Translation were too lengthy for footnotes, so they were added to an appendix (pp.797–813). Smith wrote himself into Genesis 50:33, "And that seer will I bless . . . and his name shall be called Joseph, and it shall be after the name of his father . . ."

[39]Joseph Smith, Jr., The Book of Mormon (Salt Lake City: The Church of Jesus Christ of Latter-day Saints, 1981).

[40]Smith's 1830 edition called Jesus "the Father" and Mary "the Mother of God" until the words "the Son of" were added to 1 Nephi 11:18, 21 and 13:40 in later editions. In Mosiah 21:28 and Ether 4:1 King Benjamin was later changed to King Mosiah. In spite of this, Smith claimed the Book of Mormon was the "most correct of any book on earth" (Book of Mormon, Introduction, 1981 ed.).

[41]Joseph Smith, Jr. et al., Doctrine and Covenants (Salt Lake City: The Church of Jesus Christ of Latter-day Saints, 1982).

[42]When the D & C is compared to the 1833 Book of Commandments, it is evident that several revelations have been altered by adding the Mormon priesthood. D & C 2:1–3; 5:17; 7:6–7; 13:1; 20:65–67; 27:8; 27:12; and 42:72–93 are not found in the original Book of Commandments.

[43]Joseph Smith, Jr., Pearl of Great Price (Salt Lake City: The Church of Jesus Christ of Latter-day Saints, 1982).

[44]The first vision of Smith, as recorded in the Pearl of Great Price, had a major textual change since 1851. Joseph Smith—History 1:33 originally said Nephi, not Moroni, appeared to Smith.

2. General Authorities and Continual Revelation

   a. What the current prophet speaks and writes under inspiration is also considered scripture and is binding; it may overrule any previous prophet or teaching in the Standard Works.[45]

   b. The Prophet, Apostles, and Seventies speak at annual and semi-annual conferences, where they give forth new revelations.

3. Types of Revelation

   a. Prophecy

      (1) This comprises the bulk of the Doctrine and Covenants.

      (2) E.g., the Joseph Smith History in the Pearl of Great Price predicts Smith's unfolding work as the restorer of the church.[46]

   b. Visions

      (1) Visions are recorded in parts of the Doctrine and Covenants.

      (2) The Pearl of Great Price contains Joseph Smith's visions for restoring the church.

   c. Inspired Speeches

      (1) These are conference speeches given by the General Authorities.

      (2) Most of them are restricted to the speeches of the prophet, who "speaks on behalf of the Lord to the Church"[47] (Doctrine and Covenants 21:4–5; 28:2).

   d. The Gift and Power of God to Translate

      (1) Only Joseph Smith possessed this gift.

      (2) Smith used the gift to produce the Book of Mormon, parts of the Pearl of Great Price, and the Joseph Smith Translation (Inspired Version) of the Bible.

B. *Arguments Used by Mormons to Support Their View of Authority and Scripture*

   1. The canon[48] of Scripture is not closed. According to Joseph F. Smith, the sixth prophet of the Mormon Church: "The canon of scripture is not full. God has never revealed at any time that he would cease to speak forever to men."[49]

---

[45]Most Mormons will stress the importance of the four Standard Works. Even though the current prophet effectively speaks in his prophetic office, Mormons generally refrain from considering it binding until it becomes a part of the four Standard Works (e.g., Spencer W. Kimball's revelation on the priesthood in 1978).

[46]Joseph Smith's vision of 1820 was first written in 1831, and was not published until 1842 (*Times and Seasons*, 3:706). See additional details in n. 4, Part I.

[47]See Ludlow, *Encyclopedia of Mormonism*, 3:1282. These inspired speeches reinforce current doctrines of the Standard Works more than they add new doctrines to the church.

[48]The term canon (Greek: *kanon*), which originally referred to a measurement or standard, later came to refer to the collection of divinely inspired writings called "Scripture."

[49]Joseph F. Smith, *Gospel Doctrine* (Salt Lake City: Deseret Book Co., 1977), 36.

2. Since in the past God always spoke through prophets, it is certain he will continue to speak through prophets in the future. As stated by Joseph F. Smith, "Modern revelation is necessary... If we are permitted to believe that he has spoken, we must and do believe that he continues to speak, because he is unchangeable."[50]

3. The true church cannot function without the guidance of living prophets and apostles. As Mormon apostle Bruce R. McConkie said, "These and other officers are to continue in the true Church as long as there are prospective candidates for salvation who need the guidance of such officers."[51]

4. Mormons use Scripture to support their view of authority.

   a. Psalm 102:27—This passage indicates that God will always speak in the same way as he previously did.

   b. Joel 2:28—In this verse, and its New Testament fulfillment (Acts 2:17), dreams and visions are a standard for how God communicates.

   c. Amos 3:7—(Usually only the last half of this verse is found in Mormon publications.) This verse indicates a perpetual line of prophets.

   d. Malachi 3:6—Since God does not change, he will always communicate by revelation and new scripture.

   e. Ephesians 2:20—The church is built upon the foundation of apostles and prophets, so they must continue.

   f. Ephesians 4:11–13—Special emphasis is laid upon apostles and prophets, making them perpetual living oracles.

C. *Refutation of Arguments Mormons Use to Support Their View of Authority and Scripture*

1. Concerning an Open Canon of Scripture

   a. The argument for an open canon is not proof that Mormon revelation, or any other religious work, should be part of the Bible.

      (1) One could believe in an open canon and still reject Mormon revelation, based on its contradictions and inconsistencies with the Old and New Testaments.[52]

      (2) To argue for an open canon implies that the same God who inspired the first writings will likewise inspire the latter; this

---

[50]Smith, *Gospel Doctrine*, 36.

[51]Bruce R. McConkie, *Mormon Doctrine*, 2d ed. (Salt Lake City: Bookcraft, 1966), 636.

[52]2 Nephi 25:23 says, "We know that it is by grace that we are saved, after all we can do." This contradicts the entire New Testament on grace, which denies works with grace (Eph. 2:8–9).

Alma 7:10 says that Jesus "shall be born of Mary, at Jerusalem, which is the land of our forefathers." This contradicts Matthew 2:1 which says, "Jesus was born in Bethlehem in Judea." Judea is the land, Bethlehem is the city, but Jerusalem is neither the land nor the city of Christ's birth.

Ether 1:35–36 contradicts Genesis 11:7–9, where God confounds the languages at Babel. In the book of Ether, Jerea and his companions were spared the confusion.

would require evidence within the latter writings that they are from the same God and not fraudulent, and the contradictions between Mormon scriptures and the Bible prevent such a proposition.

b. It seems unreasonable and futile for Mormons to insist upon an open biblical canon. When Joseph Smith retranslated his Bible he never added any books to its canon. The footnote for the Song of Solomon (1:1) in the Mormon edition of the Bible says, "The JST manuscript states that 'The Songs of Solomon are not inspired writings.'" This makes Joseph Smith's revision of the Bible a 65-book Mormon collection, as opposed to the 66-book Protestant collection. He rejected one book and added no others, thus closing the biblical canon. To continue arguing for an open canon is self-defeating.

2. Concerning the Argument That God Has Always Spoken Through Prophets and Must Necessarily Continue To Do So

   a. In order for Mormons to prove that a succession of prophets would continue from the Old Testament to the New Testament, they must first demonstrate that the New Testament expected such a succession, and this cannot be done.

   b. God sometimes works in his people in certain ways and then ceases when his purpose is fulfilled.

      (1) Some of the things which God used for a designated period include the Noahic flood, the manna from heaven, the ark of the covenant, the Jerusalem temple, the ceremonial sacrifices, and the Old Testament prophets.

      (2) God shows us in several New Testament verses that the role of the prophet-leader—such as the Mormons claim for their own prophets—was consummated in Jesus Christ and his forerunner, John the Baptist (Matt. 11:13; Eph. 2:20; Heb 1:1–2).

   c. Jesus, as head of the church, is our only prophet, thus ending Old Testament prophets.

      (1) Acts 3:22–23—Peter preached the living and resurrected Christ as the fulfillment of a Mosaic prophecy: "For Moses said, 'The Lord your God will raise up for you a prophet like me from among your own people; you must listen to everything he tells you. Anyone who does not listen to him will be completely cut off from among his people."

      (2) Acts 7:37—Stephen preached Jesus as this prophet: "This is that Moses who told the Israelites, 'God will send you a prophet like me from your own people.'"

   d. The gift of prophecy that was exercised in the early church is not to be confused with the prophets of the Old Testament.

(1) Ephesians 4:8–11 distinguishes the "gift of prophecy" from the prophets who were the foundation (Eph. 2:20).

(2) The gift of prophecy differs from the prophets in the Old Testament in that: it was part of the New Testament worship service (1 Cor. 14:26), both men and women prophesied (11:4–5), it was for the believers, not unbelievers (14:22), it was to be judged (14:29), it was exercised by regular members (14:31), and it was given for edification, exhortation, and comfort (14:3).

 e. God has provided heavenly guidance through means other than a prophet-leader. Jesus, as prophet, priest, and king of the church, sent the Holy Spirit to guide his people.

  (1) John 16:13—The purpose of the Holy Spirit indwelling the believer is to "guide you into all truth."

  (2) John 14:16–18—Jesus promised to provide believers with guidance from the Counselor, the Holy Spirit (vv. 16–17), not to leave us "as orphans" (v. 18).

4. Concerning the Mormon Interpretation of Biblical Passages

 a. Psalm 102:27 has nothing to do with new revelatory Scripture, but merely states that God does not change.

  (1) This text supports the Christian position and denies that of the Mormons.

  (2) The contradictions found in the Mormon scriptures portray a changeable God, not an unchangeable one. A clear example is the issue of polygamy. Mormons believe God commanded polygamy for eternity (D & C 132) but then God forbade the practice fifty years later (D & C Official Declaration—1).

 b. Joel 2:28 predicts the moving of God's Holy Spirit, which was fulfilled at Pentecost (Acts 2:16–18), not in the nineteenth century.

  (1) Peter made specific reference to this in Acts 2:16: "This is what was spoken by the prophet Joel." Peter clearly set the stage for proper interpretation when he referred to the outpouring of the Holy Spirit, the speaking in tongues, and the understanding in fifteen dialects. To apply Joel 2:32 to the revivals of nineteenth-century America is contrary to what Peter said was the proper application of this text.

  (2) The timing for the fulfillment of this prophecy is found in Joel 2:29: "in those days," the days of Pentecost.

  (3) The terminology of Joel and Acts does not fit the terminology of modern Mormonism. Joel said, "your sons and daughters shall prophesy," but in Mormonism, there is a male prophet and his two male counselors, but no prophetesses. The New

Testament gift of prophecy spans gender, teaching the legitimacy of prophetesses in Acts 21:9 and 1 Corinthians 11:5.

c. Amos 3:7 says nothing about prophets contributing additional Scripture, but speaks about prophets warning of disasters.

    (1) The context of this passage is a series of seven preceding questions leading into this verse.

    (2) In reference to those questions, God states, "Surely the Sovereign Lord does nothing without revealing his plan to his servants the prophets."

    (3) The antecedent to "does nothing" is found in verse 6: "When a trumpet sounds in a city, do not the people tremble? When disaster comes to a city, has not the Lord caused it?" As a trumpeter sounds a warning, so the Lord used prophets to warn people. Disasters can be punishments from the Lord (see v. 2); then the Lord will use a prophet to sound a warning.

d. Malachi 3:6 supports the Christian position rather than the Mormon position.

    (1) Mormons suggest that if God once gave Scripture, then he must continue giving Scripture.

    (2) Mormons quote only the first sentence in this verse and thus remove it from its context concerning the progeny of Jacob. The entire verse reads, "I the Lord do not change. So you, O descendants of Jacob, are not destroyed." God here promises Jacob that he is faithful and true in his character: He does not change and will not destroy Jacob.

e. Ephesians 2:20 does not support the Mormon view. The context clearly shows the church is presently being built upon the one foundation of apostles, prophets, and Jesus Christ. We would no sooner replace the apostles or prophets than we would Jesus. The foundation is complete.

f. Ephesians 4:11–13 presents an interesting problem for Mormons because, though they quote it in support of their church structure, it actually refutes it, since apostles precede prophets.

    (1) The ecclesiastical structure of Mormon church hierarchy is different from that listed in Ephesians 4:11.

    (2) Their order of authority begins with the prophet first, apostles second, seventies third, presiding bishops fourth, then area presidents, regional representatives, stake presidents, ward bishops, and elders.

D. The Biblical Doctrine of the Authority of Scripture

1. Authority of the Biblical Message

a. The Bible is sufficient because it is the complete message necessary for salvation.

(1) Paul told the church at Rome that his message to them is complete (Rom. 15:14, 18–19). Paul said, "I myself am convinced, my brothers, that you yourselves are full of goodness, complete in knowledge and competent to instruct one another" (v.14), and that he had "fully proclaimed the gospel of Christ" (v. 19). He further assured them that if they had lacked any knowledge, he would have given it: "I will not venture to speak of anything except what Christ has accomplished through me" (v. 18).

(2) Peter also taught that the message of the apostles was complete and sufficient for salvation. In 2 Peter 1:16 he makes a distinction between pseudo-gospels and the genuine message: "We did not follow cleverly invented stories." This shows the completeness and sufficiency of the apostolic message.

(3) Jude, the brother and servant of Jesus, urged the church to "contend for the faith that was once for all entrusted to the saints" (v. 3). It is evident that the complete message had been entrusted to the saints, and that this message was delivered once, not in a partial or incomplete manner, but all at once and once for all.

b. The Bible is sufficient because the writers wrote only the inspired words of God, no more and no less.

(1) Luke introduced his Gospel with a statement of its completeness. Luke 1:3 says "Since I myself have carefully investigated everything from the beginning, it seemed good also to me to write an orderly account for you," indicating a complete account of all necessary facts. Verse 4 satisfies the intellect with this assurance: "so that you may know the certainty of the things you have been taught." The oral tradition taught in the early church gained the certainty of an unerring text.

(2) John presented his Gospel as the complete message for eternal life. In John 19:35 he claims to be an eyewitness of the things he wrote about, and he testifies that it is true so that his readers may believe. In 20:31, John tells us that what he wrote is all we need for belief in Christ; had more been necessary for salvation, he would have written it. John 21:24–25 reiterates this by telling us that much more could have been written, but he wrote only what was necessary, and thus it stands complete.

2. Authority of the Biblical Canon

a. The Old Testament Canon

(1) The Old Testament canon, or Hebrew Scriptures, was established by the time of Christ's ministry. The Old Testament canon was known by its smaller divisions of the Law and the Prophets (Matt. 7:12) or the Law, Prophets, and Psalms (Luke

24:44). This apparently met with Christ's approval, for he referred to it and did not challenge it.

(2) Additional support for the Hebrew canon is grounded in the quotations of Jesus. He never quoted other than what we have.[53]

(3) Some say that the Jewish council of Jamnia (A.D. 90) determined the Old Testament canon, but this is not the case; the council only declared what was officially recognized by the Jews.[54]

b. The New Testament Canon

The basis for including the twenty-seven books in the New Testament is given within the New Testament.

(1) Apostolic Approval

The apostles either wrote or endorsed all the New Testament books: Matthew, John, Paul, and Peter all wrote books; Mark, Luke, James, Jude, and the writer of Hebrews received apostolic approval.[55] These writings were considered authoritative from their inception, and their internal divine guidance is recognized (Matt. 1:1; Mark 1:1; Luke 1:3; John 20:31; 1 Thess. 2:13; Heb. 1:2; James 1:1; Jude 1). Mormon revelation fails to meet the biblical standard, for no apostle wrote or authorized its text.

(2) The Consistency of the New Testament Message

The message of any particular book must be consistent with the corporate message of Scripture. Paul stressed this among those at Berea (Acts 17:11), Corinth (2 Cor. 11:4), and Galatia (Gal. 1:6–9). The Mormon scriptures soundly fail this test.

(3) The Closing of the Canon

The purpose of the Old Testament was to point to the Messiah; when the Messiah arrived there would be a natural closing of the canon because it had been fulfilled in him. The purpose of

---

[53]One could amass a library of the Jewish literature available during the time of Christ. Even the historical matter in the Apocrypha was respected by the Jewish community, but Jesus never referred to it or quoted it as Scripture.

[54]See R. T. Beckwith, "The Canon of the Old Testament," in *The Origin of the Bible*, ed. Philip Wesley Comfort (Wheaton, Ill.: Tyndale House, 1992).

[55]Mark, a companion of the apostles (Acts 13:5, here called John), is said to have written his Gospel from Peter's viewpoint (*Barnes' Notes on the New Testament*, 1 vol. [Grand Rapids: Kregel Publications, 1962], 146). Luke, another companion of the apostles (Acts 16:10), wrote from gathering eyewitness accounts (Luke 1:1–3). James, who wrote the epistle, is a brother of Jesus and was in authority with the apostles (Acts 15:13). Jude, a brother of Jesus, was received as authoritative and is referenced very early in church history by Clement of Rome (first century) and Tertullian (second century). The writer of the book of Hebrews has been under discussion since the earliest history of the church, but its authenticity and representation of the apostolic message is not disputed. (F. F. Bruce, *The Canon of Scripture* [Downers Grove, Ill.: InterVarsity Press, 1988], 130). Its writer indicates the temple is standing (10:11), and Timothy is still living (13:25), which places its date in the apostolic age, before A.D. 70.

the New Testament is to show that Jesus is the Messiah. Since Jesus adequately demonstrated his identity there is a natural closing of the New Testament because its purpose had been fulfilled.

  c. The Apostles Granted No Succession

   (1) The apostles, who died in the first century, determined what fit the message, historical time-frame, and authorship (2 Peter 3:16; 1 John 1:1–2).

   (2) The apostles gave no method beyond their death for receiving inspired Scripture, so we must conclude that they were fully satisfied with and aware of the closure of the canon.

   (3) John, the last living apostle, was satisfied that what was written was sufficient. He noted in John 20:31 that much more could have been written, but it is unnecessary because what was written is sufficient.

II. The Nature of God

A. *The Mormon View of God Briefly Stated*

  1. God the Father is an exalted man from another planet like earth.
  2. He was begotten of the species of gods, who existed before him in an infinite series of gods who were once men.
  3. He was married, died, and was resurrected to be the god of heaven.
  4. He and his goddess wife, Mother God, had millions of spirit-children in heaven; this spirit-world domain is called the preexistence.
  5. Joseph Smith taught that because the Hebrew word for "God," *Elohim*, is a plural noun, this proves that there are many gods.
  6. The image and likeness of God in man also proves that God is a man.

B. *Arguments Mormons Use to Support Their View of the Nature of God*

  1. God the Father is an exalted man.

   a. Joseph Smith taught, "The Father has a body of flesh and bones as tangible as man's." [56]

   b. The corporeal nature of the Father is derived from other gods of the same species. "After men have got their exaltations and their crowns—have become gods, even the sons of God—are made kings of kings and lords of lords, they have the power then of propagating their species in spirit."[57]

   c. Previous to the creation of this earth, the Father dwelt as a man upon another earth. As Joseph Smith states, "God himself the

---

[56]Doctrine and Covenants, 130:22.

[57]Brigham Young, *Journal of Discourses,* 26 vols. (Liverpool: The Church of Jesus Christ of Latter-day Saints, 1854–86), 6:227.

31

Father of us all, dwelt on an earth the same as Jesus Christ himself did."[58]

d. Joseph Fielding Smith taught that the Father had a mortal body that died and was resurrected: "The matter [that] seems such a mystery is the statement that our Father in heaven at one time passed through a life and death and is an exalted man."[59]

e. God the Father is married, has a goddess-wife, and produced heavenly offspring. "A Heavenly Mother shares parenthood with the Heavenly Father. This concept leads Latter-day Saints to believe that she is like him in glory, perfection, compassion, wisdom, and holiness. ... Joseph F. Smith ... teaches that 'man, as a spirit, was begotten and born of heavenly parents.' ... Though the scriptures contain only hints, statements from presidents of the church over the years indicated that human beings have a Heavenly Mother as well as a Heavenly Father."[60]

2. There is an infinite number of gods.

a. Joseph Smith described the infinite series of previous gods: "If Jesus Christ was the Son of God, and John [the Apostle] discovered that God the Father of Jesus Christ had a Father, you may suppose that He had a Father also. Where was there ever a son without a father? And where was there ever a father without first being a son?"[61]

b. Joseph Smith taught the plurality of gods is based upon the Hebrew: "In the very beginning the Bible shows there is a plurality of Gods beyond the power of refutation. ... The word *Elohim* ought to be in the plural all the way through—Gods. The heads of the Gods appointed one God for us; and when you take view of the subject, it sets one free to see all the beauty, holiness and perfection of the Gods."[62]

3. Men are created in the image of God's body.

a. The Book of Moses (9:5–6) says that man was made in the image of God's body: "In the day that God created man, in the likeness of God made he him; in the image of his own body, male and female, created he them."

b. While males were made like the Heavenly Father's body, females were made like the Heavenly Mother's body.

(1) Seventies member Milton Hunter wrote, "Thus males were created in the image and likeness of God the Eternal Father

[58]*Journal of Discourses,* 6:3.

[59]Joseph Fielding Smith, *Doctrines of Salvation,* 3 vols. (Salt Lake City: Bookcraft, 1956), 1:10.

[60]Elaine A. Cannon, "Mother in Heaven," in Ludlow, *Encyclopedia of Mormonism,* 4:961.

[61]Smith, *Documentary History of the Church,* 6:476. See also McConkie, *Mormon Doctrine,* 576.

[62]Joseph Fielding Smith, *Teachings of the Prophet Joseph Smith* (Salt Lake City: Deseret Book Co., 1976), 372.

while the females were formed in the image and likeness of their Eternal Mother."[63]

    (2) Prophet Spencer W. Kimball elaborates upon this theme: "God made man in his own image and certainly he made woman in the image of his wife-partner."[64]

4. Mormons use Scripture (KJV) to support their view of God.

    a. Genesis 1:1 and subsequent passages illustrate the plurality of gods with the plural noun *Elohim*, which may be translated "gods."

    b. Genesis 1:26–27

        (1) This verse depicts God and Adam as having the same image and likeness.

        (2) We know what Adam looks like, so God must look the same.

    c. Genesis 5:1–3

        (1) Adam was created in the image and likeness of God, so God looks like Adam.

        (2) Seth was begotten in the image and likeness of Adam, so Seth looked like Adam and Adam looked like God.

    d. Genesis 32:30

        (1) Jacob saw God "face to face" (see also Ex. 33:11); therefore God must have a body.

        (2) Jacob's emphasis upon God's face shows he has a body.

    e. Exodus 33:23

        (1) This verse mentions God's "hand" and "back," showing that his nature is similar to man's.

        (2) Moses was permitted to see God, so God has a physical nature.

    f. Deuteronomy 10:17

        In order for God to be "God of gods" there must be a plurality of gods (see also Ps. 136:2).

    g. John 8:17–18

        (1) It takes the witness of two men for something to be true.

        (2) By using the Father as a second witness, Jesus is saying that the Father is a man.

    h. John 14:9

        Jesus had a physical body like the Father's.

    i. Acts 17:28

        God and his wife literally begat us in heaven, as spirit progeny.

    j. 1 Corinthians 8:5

        There is a plurality of gods in heaven and earth.

---

[63]Milton Hunter, *Pearl of Great Price Commentary* (Salt Lake City: Bookcraft, 1951), 114.

[64]Edward L. Kimball, comp., *Teachings of the Prophet Spencer W. Kimball* (Salt Lake City: Bookcraft, 1983), 25.

k. Hebrews 12:9

        (1) We have our fathers on earth, and so we must have a Father of our spirits in heaven; the fathers on earth begat us in the flesh, so the Father in heaven must have begotten us in the spirit.

        (2) The Father of our spirits must have a partner just as the fathers of our flesh do, hence, our heavenly Mother.[65]

C. *Refutation of Arguments Mormons Use to Support Their View of the Nature of God*

    1. The way in which Joseph Smith attempted to translate *Elohim* disregards the most elementary principles of Hebrew grammar.

        a. When *Elohim* is used of the true God it is usually joined with a singular verb, which renders the plural noun as the singular, God; when speaking of false gods, *Elohim* is always joined with a plural verb.

           (1) Theologian Geerhardus Vos said, "*Elohim* is simply a plural expressing majesty, magnitude, fullness, richness.... The Hebrew sometimes has to use it as a true numerical plural, e.g., when speaking of pagan gods. In such a case, however, it is always construed with a plural verb, whereas in a case of reference to the true God it takes a singular verb."[66]

           (2) The Septuagint (250 B.C.), which is the Greek translation of the Hebrew Old Testament, shows us that the Hebrews understood that the plural noun *Elohim* was to be translated as the singular noun "God."

        b. The Mormon apostle Bruce R. McConkie says that *Elohim* is also the personal name for the Father.[67] This creates significant problems for the Mormon position.

           (1) The first problem involves translating the Father's name. Smith said *Elohim* should be translated "gods." McConkie said *Elohim* is the Father's personal name. Yet they never translate his name as "gods"; their inconsistent and arbitrary usage attempts to avoid uncomfortable situations that contradict their beliefs.

           (2) Mormons have no consistent rule they can apply to determine when the word *Elohim* means the Father and when it refers to gods or pagan deities.

           (3) *Elohim* cannot be strictly applied as a name for the Father. Mormons claim that *Elohim* is the personal name for the

---

[65]The subject of Mother God is delicate among Mormons and is not widely discussed. Some Mormons say the subject is too sacred to discuss deeply.

[66]Geerhardus Vos, *Biblical Theology: Old and New Testaments* (Grand Rapids: Eerdmans, 1948), 65.

[67]McConkie, *Mormon Doctrine*, 224.

Father, while Jehovah is the personal name for the Son and yet we find that *Elohim* is used of the Son (Heb. 1:8 quoting Ps. 45:6 and Heb. 1:10–11 quoting Ps. 102:24–26). We also find Jehovah, which Mormons use strictly of Jesus, applied to the Father (Isa. 63:16).

The compound name *Jehovah-Elohim* (Gen. 2:4; Ex. 3:15, 18; 4:5; 5:1; 7:5; 34:6) presents an even greater problem for Mormons because distinction of the two names disappears. Instead of supporting Mormonism, the compound name *Jehovah-Elohim* strongly supports the unity and oneness of Jehovah-God, particularly since it is used only with singular verbs.

Further proof that *Elohim* cannot be the personal name for the Father is its other Hebrew usages: *Elohim* is used for false gods about 240 times (Gen. 31:30, 32), for false goddesses (1 Kings 11:5, 33), for judges (Ex. 21:6; 22:8, 9), and for angels (Ps. 8:5).

2. The terms "image" and "likeness" do not mean that human beings have godlike bodies. The image of God is declared as invisible in Colossians 1:15.

a. Dr. James Orr summarizes biblical thought on the image of God in humanity:

"In Gen. 1:26–27, the truth is declared that God created man in His own 'image', after His 'likeness'. The two ideas denote the same thing—resemblance to God. The like conception of man, tacit or avowed, underlies all revelation. . . . It lies in the nature of the case that the 'image' does not consist in bodily form; it can only reside in spiritual qualities, in man's mental and moral attributes as a self-conscious, rational, personal agent, capable of self-determination and obedience to moral law. . . . The image of God, defaced but not entirely lost through sin, is restored in yet more perfect form in the redemption of Christ."[68]

b. God's image in human beings is not physical; the spiritual but fallen human nature needs to be conformed to the image and likeness of God through Christ Jesus.

(1) Romans 8:29—"Those God foreknew he also predestined to be conformed to the likeness of his Son."

(2) 1 Corinthians 15:49—"Just as we have borne the likeness of the earthly man, we shall also bear the image of the heavenly."

(3) Colossians 3:10—"Put on the new self, which is being renewed in knowledge in the image of its Creator."

---

[68]James Orr, ed., *The International Standard Bible Encyclopedia*, 5 vols. (Chicago: Howard-Severance Company, 1915), 2:1264.

   c. God made both men and women after his image and likeness, which prevents the image from being physical.

      (1) Genesis 1:27 says, "In the image of God he created him; male and female he created them."

      (2) The image of God is shared by both male and female, which necessitates a spiritual nature.

      (3) The Mormon idea that God used his wife as a model for Eve ranks with mythological conjectures. It disregards the fact that both male and female reflect the image of God, and lacks any biblical support whatsoever.

3. An infinite number of gods prior to God the Father is impossible.

   a. There is no first in an infinite line and, if there is no first, there is no beginning.[69]

   b. If Mormons claim there was a first god somewhere, they must then resolve several problems.

      (1) The infinite lineage of gods is simply reduced to a very large but finite number.

      (2) The god at the beginning of a finite line of gods would be unique in this succession of gods, and in fact greater in his existence, since he did not come from a line of gods.

      (3) The first god in this large number of gods did not derive his source from another, and therefore always existed without cause.

      (4) If Mormons ever concede that an uncaused God exists, then they will have destroyed Mormon exaltation, because a unique, infinite God would exist above all of their finite gods.

4. Mormons misuse Scripture to support their view of God.

   a. Genesis 1:1—Although biblical scholars have explored the meaning of *Elohim* over the years, none have concurred with Mormonism's neglect of the singular verb (*bara*) or have translated *Elohim* as "gods."

   b. Genesis 1:26–27 shows that the image and likeness of God was given to both Adam and Eve. This limits the meaning to the spiritual nature, since the physical nature of men and women differ.

   c. Genesis 5:1–4 supports the Christian doctrine that all are born under Adam's sin (Rom. 5:12, 18). Seth inherited Adam's spiritual image, which was a fallen, sinful nature.

---

[69]For a well-developed philosophical argument against the Mormon concept of God, see Francis J. Beckwith and Stephen E. Parrish, *The Mormon Concept of God: A Philosophical Analysis* (Lewiston, N.Y.: Edwin Mellen, 1991).

d. Genesis 32:30 is one of many "theophanies" (appearances of God) in the Old Testament.[70]

    (1) There were several occasions in the Old Testament when God appeared in some concrete form, such as a burning bush (Ex. 3:1–4), an angel (Judg. 6:22), or human form (Gen. 18:1–2).

    (2) Appearances of God in human form were temporary, and they no more make him a man than appearing as a burning bush makes him a shrub.

    (3) Many biblical scholars believe that all theophanies were appearances of Jesus Christ before he was born to Mary. This view is based upon John 1:18 and 6:46, where we find that no one has seen the Father. In 12:37–41 John quotes Isaiah (6:10) and says Isaiah saw Christ and his glory.

    (4) Theophanies do not support the Mormon position of an anthropomorphic God since it was the preincarnate Christ who appeared in the Old Testament.

e. Exodus 33:20–33 is another theophany (see the preceding discussion).

f. When Deuteronomy 10:17 describes God as the greatest of all so-called lords or gods, this does not suggest that there are other true gods or lords, but rather that the true God is above all the gods of human design.

g. John 14:7–9 does not teach that God the Father has a physical body.

    (1) Jesus said of the Father, "From now on, you do know him and have seen him" (v. 7); the disciples knew they had not seen anything physical, hence their response, "Lord, show us the Father" (v. 8).

    (2) Jesus answered them, "Anyone who has seen me has seen the Father. How can you say, 'Show us the Father'?" (v. 9).

    (3) The disciples saw the Father by looking at what Jesus had done (vv. 9–11), referring to the Son's moral likeness to the Father, not to a physical body for the Father.

h. In Acts 17:28 Paul quotes the Greek poets Aratus and Cleanthes as saying "We are his offspring."

    (1) Paul made use of other pagan writings such as Epimenides in the same verse, "In him we live and move and have our being" (see also Titus 1:12). With this, Paul indicates God's omnipresence and invisible nature.

---

[70]Studies on theophanies may be found in any good Bible dictionary, Bible encyclopedia, or a book on basic doctrine. See Merrill C. Tenney, ed., *Zondervan Pictorial Encyclopedia of the Bible*, 5 vols. (Grand Rapids: Zondervan, 1975–76).

(2) Paul is not saying God inspired the poets' writings, but simply acknowledging a measure of agreement between their writing and God's truth.

(3) Creation, not procreation, is Paul's subject. Paul has already declared God as the creator of all things (v. 24). The correct understanding of the term "offspring" is found in this context: God gives life to all people as the natural progeny of Adam.

  i. 1 Corinthians 8:5 refutes the polytheism found in Mormonism.

(1) The words "so-called gods" (v. 5) is not a recognition of other gods, but a denial that any such gods exist.

(2) When Paul calls these gods and lords "so-called," he is mocking the possibility of their existence.

  j. Hebrews 12:9 does not say that God begat spirit-children in heaven.

(1) A contrast is drawn between our earthly father's discipline and our heavenly Father's discipline.

(2) If we respect our earthly fathers because of their discipline, we should all the more submit to God when he disciplines us.

(3) Hebrews was written to Jewish converts to Christianity, so "Father of our spirits" refers to being born again. James 1:18 says that we are begotten by God through "the word of truth." First Peter 1:23 says that we are "born again" through the "word of God." There is no sexual procreation by the gods to produce spirit-children; we become his children through God's Word.

D. The Biblical Doctrine on the Nature of God

1. Scripture teaches monotheism.

  a. Polytheism is repeatedly renounced in the Bible.

(1) Genesis 1:1—The opening verse of the Bible declares the truth of one God. (The Hebrew is translated as a singular noun, based on the singular verb.) He is the uncreated Creator; nothing existed with him in the beginning.

(2) The theme of one God is carried on throughout the Bible (Deut. 32:39; Ps. 86:10; Isa. 43:10, 44:6, 45:21).

  b. Other so-called gods are not gods by nature.

(1) Paul refers to the false gods as not true by nature: "When you did not know God, you were slaves to those who by nature are not gods" (Gal. 4:8).

(2) All other gods are the product of human imagination. Paul said we ought not think that God is "an image made by man's design and skill" (Acts 17:29) and thereby exchange "the glory of the immortal God for images made to look like mortal man"

(Rom. 1:23). Mormons will argue correctly that these are idols. However, when Mormons paint pictures of the First Vision accounts of Joseph Smith with two human-gods appearing in a light, these are no less images. Thus, both the Romans and the Mormons have exchanged God's heavenly likeness for an earthly likeness. Isaiah summed up the issue with the challenge, "To whom, then, will you compare God? What image will you compare him to?" (40:18). This rhetorical question has the built-in answer, "None." Nothing can adequately be compared to God. Adam is not a good comparison, nor is any figure of a man, painted or carved.

2. God is spirit.

   a. The Bible teaches that God's nature is spirit (John 4:24; 2 Cor. 3:17).

     (1) Since God is the Creator of all things (Gen. 1:1; John 1:3; Col. 1:16–17), he cannot be made of material substance.

     (2) God is a personal, infinite, self-existent, immaterial, transcendent being who derives no attribute from another source.

   b. God does not have a spirit, as if it were a component of many other parts. He is pure spirit.

3. God is not a man.

   a. Numbers 23:19 states, "God is not a man, that he should lie."

   b. Hosea 11:9 says, "I am God, and not man—the Holy One among you."

III. The Trinity

A. *The Mormon View of the Trinity Briefly Stated*

   1. There are three gods who are perfect in knowledge, power, and glory.[71]

   2. The Father, Son, and Holy Ghost have three distinct bodies, although the Holy Spirit currently has only a spirit-body; their distinct bodily existence prevents them from being one in nature or essence.

   3. Their oneness is in purpose, thought, and will.

   4. The word *Godhead* is synonymous with *Trinity*, and relates to the purpose of the three, not to their nature.

B. *Mormon Arguments Used to Support Their Position on the Trinity*

   1. Each god is born as a man and later progresses to the level of godhood. The Father, Son, and Holy Ghost, as distinct and separate entities born at different times and in different places, became gods at different times in different worlds.

---

[71]Note: The Mormon definition of *Trinity* is tritheistic (three gods). This is not the orthodox Christian definition, which is one God in three persons.

2. The Godhead is three gods working for the same purpose.
   a. John A. Widtsoe wrote, "This revealed doctrine of the composition and nature of the Godhead teaches that there are at least three Gods."[72]
   b. James Talmage said, "The unity of the Godhead was a oneness of perfection in purpose, plan, and action, as the scriptures declare it to be, and not an impossible union of personalities, as generations of false teachers had tried to impress."[73]
3. The doctrine of one God in three persons is to be denied, and the word Trinity is to be used to represent three gods.
   a. Apostle Bruce R. McConkie teaches, "We hear the voice of false Christs when we hear the Athanasian Creed proclaim that 'whosoever will be saved' must believe that the Father, Son, and Holy Ghost are incomprehensible and uncreated, that they form a Trinity of equals...."[74]
   b. Joseph Smith denied outright the orthodox Christian doctrine of the Trinity: "Many men say there is one God; the Father, the Son and the Holy Ghost are only one God! I say that is a strange God anyhow—three in one, and one in three! It is a curious organization....All are to be crammed into one God, according to sectarianism. It would make the biggest God in all the world. He would be a wonderfully big God—he would be a giant or a monster."[75]
4. *Elohim* and Jehovah are the personal names of the Father and the Son, respectively. Talmage said, "*Elohim*, as understood and used in the restored Church of Jesus Christ, is the name-title of God the Eternal Father, whose firstborn Son in the spirit is Jehovah—the Only Begotten in the flesh, Jesus Christ."[76]
5. Mormons believe the Bible teaches that there are three gods in the Godhead.
   a. Genesis 1:26—This verse contains the words "us" and "our," which shows that there is more than one god.
   b. Matthew 28:19—Jesus used the names "Father, Son, and Holy Spirit," showing more than one god.
   c. John 1:1—There were two gods in the beginning, the Father and the Son.
   d. John 5:19—When Jesus said that "whatever the Father does the Son also does" he meant that they have the same purpose.

[72]John A. Widtsoe, *Evidences and Reconciliation* (Salt Lake City: Bookcraft, 1960), 65.

[73]James Talmage, *Jesus the Christ* (Salt Lake City: Deseret Book Co., 1962), 374.

[74]Bruce R. McConkie, *The Millennial Messiah* (Salt Lake City: Deseret Book Co., 1980), 48.

[75]Smith, *Documentary History of the Church*, 6:476.

[76]Talmage, *Jesus the Christ*, 38.

e. John 8:17–18—By identifying the two male witnesses with himself and the Father, Jesus showed that the Father is also a man and that they are united in purpose.

f. Acts 7:55–56—Before Stephen was stoned he saw two beings, the Father and Son.

C. Refutation of Arguments Mormons Use to Support Their View of the Trinity

1. The Hebrew words *Elohim* and *Jehovah* are not personal names for the Father and Son.

   a. The word *Elohim* is a general word for God and may be used of pagan gods as well as the true God (Gen. 31:30, 32; cf. v.19).

   b. The word *Jehovah* is a specific name for God and is never used of any others.

   c. The two words are often combined as *Jehovah-Elohim*, which refutes the idea that they are personal names for two entities (Gen. 2:4; Ex. 34:6).

      (1) If anything, the combined name *Jehovah-Elohim* shows the unity of God.

      (2) Deuteronomy 6:4 literally says, "Hear, O Israel, Jehovah our *Elohim* is one Jehovah," which shows the inseparable unity in God's nature.

2. The Bible uses the word *Godhead* to describe the full essence of God.

   a. The term *Godhead* refers to the essence of God, not to the idea that there are three gods working for one purpose.

   b. There are three New Testament occurrences of "Godhead" (KJV).

      (1) Acts 17:29—Here "Godhead" is better translated "the divine" (NIV), which is the common Greek usage.

      (2) Romans 1:20—Paul uses the Greek word *theiotes* (Godhead, KJV; better translated as "divine nature," NIV), to describe the full attributes of God.

      (3) Colossians 2:9—Paul uses the Greek word *theotetos* (Godhead, KJV) to describe "Deity" (NIV), which includes the fullness of God's nature.

3. Smith's idea that the Trinity is the Father, Son, and Holy Spirit "all crammed into one," reveals his lack of knowledge about the unity of the three divine persons as one God.

   a. Christianity teaches that there is one God.

   b. Within the nature of this one God are three persons, namely, Father, Son, and Holy Spirit.

   c. Each person shares in all the nature and attributes of God, so we do not have three gods; we have one God who exists as three divine persons.

41

d. The three persons have distinction as to identity—they can say "I" of themselves and "he" of the other persons—yet they share one essence or nature, that is, the divine nature.

e. There is a oneness to the three persons, but the oneness centers upon the one nature of God; each person does not possess a separate divine nature of his own, but one and the same divine essence.

f. At the same time Christians do not deny that the three persons of the Trinity are one in purpose, for the three persons could hardly be one God and not have the same purpose.

    (1) Mormons limit the oneness of the Godhead to purpose and will.

    (2) This is because they see the Godhead as three gods with one purpose instead of three persons within one God.

g. The oneness in essence of the three persons is shown by the fact that they all possess the same attributes that apply exclusively to the one true God.

    (1) God is the only eternal being: Father (Isa. 40:28), Son (John 1:1), and Holy Spirit (Heb. 9:14).

    (2) God is the only omnipotent being: Father (Jer. 32:17), Son (1 Cor. 1:24), and Holy Spirit (Luke 1:35–37).

    (3) God is the only omnipresent being: Father (1 Kings 8:27), Son (Matt. 18:20), and Holy Spirit (Ps. 139:7–10).

    (4) God is the only omniscient being: Father (Isa. 46:10), Son (Col. 2:3), and Holy Spirit (Isa. 40:13).

4. Mormons misuse texts referring to the Godhead.

a. Matthew 28:19

    (1) This text supports the doctrine of the Trinity, not the Mormon notion of three gods.

    (2) The singular noun *name* for the Father, Son, and Holy Spirit shows that all three persons have one name, not three names for three entities.

    (3) The word *name* also connotes the full authority of the triune God. The context (v. 18) is authority: "All authority in heaven and on earth has been given to me. Therefore go. . . . " The Greek grammarian A. T. Robertson says, "The use of name (*onoma*) here is a common one in the Septuagint and the papyri for power or authority."[77] The word *name* is used elsewhere in Scripture for authority (e.g., Acts 4:7).

b. John 1:1—While this verse clearly distinguishes the persons of the Father and Son, it in no way implies that there are two gods.

---

[77]A. T. Robertson, *Word Pictures in the New Testament,* 6 vols. (Nashville: Broadman Press, 1930), 1:245.

(1) The clause, "and the Word was God," shows that Jesus has the same essence or nature as the Father.

(2) "The Word" (Greek: *ho logos*) carries the definite article, which identifies it as the subject, and "God" (*theos*) carries no definite article, identifying it as the predicate.[78] Since the predicate expresses something about the subject, we can see why "God" (the predicate) tells us something about "the Word" (the subject), namely, that "the Word was God." Jamison, Fausset, and Brown's commentary adds, "It was not the distinctness and the fellowship of *another being*, as if there were *more Gods than one*, but of One who was *Himself God*—in such sense that the *absolute unity* of the Godhead, the great principle of all religion, is only transferred from the region of shadowy abstraction to the region of essential life and love."[79]

c. John 5:19

(1) This text shows the unity of the Father and Son in the work of the Son.

(2) The Father and Son are "doing" (present tense) one work together.

d. John 8:17–18

(1) The context of verses 14–16 is judgment, so Jesus introduces the law to support his claim.

(2) Verse 16 is crucial to correctly understanding the passage, "But if I do judge, my decisions are right, because I am not alone. I stand with the Father, who sent me." Here Jesus removes himself from judgment by earthly judges (Pharisees) and appeals to the highest source, saying he and the Father are in perfect agreement. Then he points out to the Pharisees (v. 17) that their law tells them it takes two testimonies to establish a fact. By pointing to the law Jesus is not saying the Father is a man any more than he is saying that the Pharisees could subpeona the Father. The Pharisees would have no right to call upon the Father as a witness, but Jesus does. In verse 18 Jesus does just that when he tells them that the Father is his other witness. By the Pharisaic standard the witness had to be credible and could only testify for himself if he had a corroborating second witness.[80] Here, Jesus supplies the Father as an irrefutable second witness.

---

[78]Robertson, *Word Pictures in the New Testament*, 1:4–5.

[79]Robert Jamieson, A. R. Fausset, and David Brown, *Commentary Practical and Explanatory on the Whole Bible* (Grand Rapids: Zondervan, 1977), 1026.

[80]Alfred Edersheim, *The Life and Times of Jesus the Messiah*, 2 vols. (Grand Rapids: Eerdmans, 1883; one vol. edition, 1971), 2:169.

e. Acts 7:55–56—This passage does not say that Stephen saw two beings, but only that he saw "the glory of God, and Jesus standing at the right hand of God."

(1) Stephen saw one body, identified as the resurrected body of Jesus.

(2) Stephen did not say, "I see two beings, God and Jesus," or "I see the Father and Jesus." Since God is Father, Son, and Holy Spirit, only the glory of God was seen along with Jesus. Even granting Mormon polytheism, the Mormons read too much into this text if they believe that Stephen saw the Father, who is not mentioned. In their theology of many gods, how can they assure us that it was not the Holy Ghost, or perhaps the grandfather-god of Jesus, instead of the Father? They cannot because the only description given is "glory," which does not mean "body."

D. The Biblical Doctrine of the Trinity

1. There is only one true God (Deut. 6:4; Isa. 43:10, 45:5; Mark 12:32; James 2:19).

2. We use the word *person* to describe three distinct centers of identity, emotion, and will.

   a. The Father uses "I" to speak of himself (John 12:28).

   b. The Son uses "I" to speak of himself (John 8:58).

   c. The Holy Spirit uses "I" to speak of himself (Acts 13:2).

3. The Father is called God (Rom. 1:7; 1 Cor. 1:3).

4. The Son is called God (Isa. 9:6; Matt. 1:23; John 1:1; 5:18; 20:28; Phil. 2:6–8; Heb. 1:8; 1 John 5:20; Rev. 1:8).

5. The Holy Spirit is called God (2 Sam. 23:2–3; Acts 5:1–4; 28:25–27; Heb. 3:7–19; 10:15–16).

6. All three persons share the nature of one God (Matt. 28:19).

IV. Christ: His Preexistence

A. The Mormon View of the Preexistence of Christ Briefly Stated

1. Only four things are eternal, absolute, and without beginning: matter, the law of progression, the priesthood, and intelligence.

2. Jesus' existence began as organized intelligence, a spirit-element that eternally exists with matter.

3. Jesus was then born as a spirit-child of Heavenly Parents, namely the Father and his wife.

4. Jesus was the firstborn of all other spirit-children, including Lucifer, Adam, and all humanity.

B. Mormon Arguments for Their Position on the Preexistence of Christ

1. Jesus began as organized intelligence. Bruce R. McConkie explained, "Implicit in his spirit birth as the Firstborn is the fact that, as with all the spirit children of the Father, he had a beginning; there was a day when he came into being as a conscious identity, as a spirit entity, as an organized intelligence."[81]

2. Jesus' eternal nature is not unique. McConkie qualified Jesus' eternal nature by saying, "How then is he the Eternal One? It might be said that he is eternal, as all men are, meaning that spirit element—the intelligence which was organized into intelligences—has always existed and is therefore eternal."[82]

3. Jesus was begotten twice of the Father: once in heaven and once on earth. Apostle James Talmage said, "Jesus Christ is the Son of *Elohim* both as spiritual and bodily offspring; that is to say, *Elohim* is literally the Father of the spirit of Jesus Christ and also of the body in which Jesus Christ performed His mission in the flesh."[83]

4. Jesus is related to Lucifer. Milton Hunter wrote about Jesus' relationship to Lucifer: "The appointment of Jesus to be the Savior of the world was contested by one of the other sons of God. He was called Lucifer, son of the morning. . . . This spirit-brother of Jesus desperately tried to become the Savior of mankind."[84]

5. Mormons use Scripture to support their view of the nature and preexistence of Christ.

    a. Job 1:6; 38:7

       (1) These texts speak of the "sons of God" (KJV) in heaven, who represent the children of the heavenly parents.

       (2) They are spirit-offspring, of whom Jesus was the first.

    b. Rev. 12:8

       (1) There was in the preexistent heaven a great war between Michael (who fought for Jesus) and the dragon (Lucifer, who lost the battle).

       (2) Lucifer, together with his warriors, was cast to the earth as Satan.

C. Refutation of the Mormon Position on the Preexistence of Christ

1. Jesus, the Son of God, did not begin as organized intelligence in the preexistence.

---

[81]Bruce R. McConkie, *The Promised Messiah* (Salt Lake City: Bookcraft, 1978), 165.

[82]McConkie, *The Promised Messiah,* 165.

[83]James Talmage, *Articles of Faith* (Salt Lake City: The Church of Jesus Christ of Latter-day Saints, 1974), 466.

[84]Milton Hunter, *Gospel Through the Ages* (Salt Lake City: Stevens and Wallis, 1945), 15.

a. The concept of an endless series of intelligences commits the same fallacy of infinite regression as in the Mormon doctrine of an infinite succession of gods (see section II.C.3. above). If one begins with a Jesus who was organized intelligence, it pushes the argument back to his Father who began as organized intelligence, which pushes it back to his father who began as organized intelligence, and so on.

b. Such a series of intelligences (organized spirit entities) cannot account for a beginning to the chain, which, since it is infinite, means there is no real beginning.

(1) A series which has no beginning is not a true series, but an illusion that breaks down when carried to its logical conclusion.

(2) Without a true beginning to the series, the series of intelligences lack any validity for its succession.

2. The idea that Jesus and Lucifer are spirit-brothers is refuted on the basis of monotheism.

a. Mormonism requires a god and goddess to produce spirit offspring.

b. The biblical teaching that there is only one God refutes the notion of many gods (see section II.D.1. above).

3. The Mormon Interpretation of Scripture is based on misinterpretation.

a. Job 1:6 and 38:7 are translated properly as "sons of God" (NIV note) or "angels" (NIV text), which is based on the plural noun *Elohim* with a plural verb.

(1) It is speaking of finite, created beings who dwell in heaven.

(2) According to Colossians 1:16, all beings in heaven are acts of creation: "For by him all things were created: things in heaven and on earth, visible and invisible."

(3) The misunderstanding in Mormonism concerns how the word *created* is interpreted.

Mormons interpret it to mean *procreated*, as in a natural sexual encounter where offspring are produced. This, however, does violence to the teaching of Colossians 1:16–17, for not all things mentioned in this text fit their description of procreation. Because there is no guideline in Mormonism for when *created* should be used in place of *procreated*, it becomes a merely arbitrary decision. Brent A. Barlow's article, "Procreation" demonstrates this loose definition: "Using the power of procreation does not alienate one from God. Rather, properly used, it enables mortals to become cocreators with him in the divine plan of salvation."[85]

---

[85]Ludlow, *Encyclopedia of Mormonism*, 3:1158.

b. Revelation 12:8 has nothing to do with spirit-brothers or councils of gods, and its context rules out such an application.

D. **The Biblical Doctrine of the Preexistence of Christ**

1. Jesus preexisted as the Creator of all things, hence he is uncreated.

   a. John 1:3; Colossians 1:16–17; and Hebrews 1:3.

   b. As the Creator of all things, Jesus could not be a spirit-born brother to Lucifer.

      (1) Lucifer is a created being (Ezek. 28:13–15).

      (2) Jesus, then, is Lucifer's creator, not his brother.

2. Jesus preexisted eternally as God, with no beginning (John 1:1; Micah 5:2; Colossians 1:17–19; Hebrews 1:8; 13:8; and 1 John 1:1).

V. Christ: His Earthly Life and Exaltation

A. **The Mormon Position on Christ's Earthly Life and Exaltation Briefly Stated**

1. Jesus was the natural child of God the Father and Mary.

2. The Holy Ghost was active but was not the agent in the conception of Jesus Christ.

3. The Father, an exalted man, sired Jesus as any man would through sexual intercourse with Mary.

4. Jesus enjoyed marriage to at least three wives before his crucifixion.

5. Jesus had children through his wives.

6. After his resurrection Jesus received the fullness of Godhood.

B. **Mormon Arguments for Their View of Christ's Life and Exaltation**

1. Jesus was not conceived by the Holy Ghost. Brigham Young laid down this doctrine for Mormons: "When the Virgin Mary conceived the child Jesus, the Father had begotten him in his own likeness. He was not begotten by the Holy Ghost."[86]

2. The Father sired Jesus.

   a. Brigham Young

   "The man Joseph, the husband of Mary, did not, that we know of, have more than one wife, but Mary the wife of Joseph had another husband.... That very babe that was cradled in the manger, was begotten, not by Joseph, the husband of Mary, but by another Being. Do you inquire by whom? He was begotten by God our heavenly Father."[87]

---

[86]Young, *Journal of Discourses,* 1:50. This sermon by Young also states that Adam is God and was the literal father of Jesus Christ.

[87]*Journal of Discourses,* 11:268.

b. Prophet Ezra Taft Benson

"The Church of Jesus Christ of Latter-day Saints proclaims that Jesus Christ is the Son of God in the most literal sense. The body in which He performed His mission in the flesh was sired by that same Holy Being we worship as God, our Eternal Father. Jesus was not the son of Joseph, nor was He begotten by the Holy Ghost. He is the Son of the Eternal Father."[88]

c. Apostle James Talmage

"That Child to be born of Mary was begotten of *Elohim*, the Eternal Father, not in violation of natural law but in accordance with a higher manifestation thereof; and, the offspring from that association of supreme sanctity, celestial Sireship."[89]

3. Jesus was a polygamist and had children.

   a. Polygamy caused the persecution and crucifixion of Jesus. Apostle Jedediah M. Grant remarked, "The grand reason of the burst of public sentiment in anathemas upon Christ and his disciples, causing his crucifixion, was evidently based upon polygamy, according to the testimony of the philosophers who rose in that age. A belief in the doctrine of a plurality of wives caused the persecution of Jesus and his followers. We might almost think they were 'Mormons.'"[90]

   b. Apostle Orson Hyde spoke about Jesus' marriage and children. ". . . I said, in my lecture on Marriage, at our last Conference, that Jesus Christ was married at Cana of Galilee, that Mary, Martha, and others were his wives, and that he begot children."[91]

   c. Brigham Young said that Abraham's promise of children was bestowed upon Jesus. "The Lord, however, gave him [Abraham] this promise, '. . . I will give you a promise that you shall yet have a posterity, and it shall multiply upon the face of the earth . . . and to their increase there shall be no end.' The same blessing was promised to the Lord Jesus Christ."[92]

4. Jesus was resurrected and was exalted to full Godhood.

   a. Prophet Joseph Fielding Smith wrote, "Christ gained fullness after [His] resurrection. The Savior did not have a fullness at first, but after he received his body and the resurrection all power was given unto him both in heaven and in earth. Although he was a God, even the Son of God, with power and authority to create this earth and other earths, yet there were some things lacking which he did not

---

[88] Ezra Taft Benson, *Teachings of the Prophet Ezra Taft Benson* (Salt Lake City: Bookcraft, 1988), 7.

[89] Talmage, *Jesus the Christ*, 81.

[90] *Journal of Discourses*, 1:346.

[91] *Journal of Discourses*, 2:210.

[92] *Journal of Discourses*, 2:301.

receive until after his resurrection. In other words he had not received the fullness until he got a resurrected body, and the same is true with those who through faithfulness become sons of God. Our bodies are essential to the fullness and the continuation of the seeds forever."[93]

b. Joseph Smith spoke about Jesus taking the Father's place: "'I shall present it [Christ's kingdom] to my Father, so that he may obtain kingdom upon kingdom, and it will exalt him in glory. He will then take a higher exaltation, and I will take his place, and thereby become exalted myself.' So that Jesus treads in the tracks of his Father, and inherits what God did before; and God is thus glorified and exalted in the salvation and exaltation of all his children."[94]

5. Mormons use Scripture to support the physical sireship, marriage, and exaltation of Jesus.

a. John 1:14 (also 1:18; 3:16)—The words "only begotten Son" (KJV, NIV note) indicate that Jesus was the literal begotten Son of the Father through Mary, in a husband and wife act of procreation.

b. John 2:1–11—The wedding at Cana in Galilee is one of the weddings where Jesus took a Jewish bride.

c. Isaiah 53:10—The words "he shall see his seed" (KJV) speak of the Messiah, and therefore, the Messiah will have children.

C. Refutation of the Mormon Concept of Jesus' Life and Exaltation

1. Scripture teaches that Mary was not married to God and did not have a child of his "sireship."

a. Matthew explicitly said that Mary was a virgin and remained a virgin until Jesus was born (Matt. 1:18, 20, 25).

b. Luke's account gives a strong testimony, from a variety of sources, that Mary was a virgin even after the child was conceived (Luke 1:26–45).

c. It is impossible to understand how Mary could have been a virgin in the Mormon doctrine.

2. The fact that the Holy Spirit was the agent in the miraculous conception of Jesus does not usurp the Father's position.

a. Just as the Father created the worlds through the Son (Heb. 1:2), and there is no conflict, so also the Holy Spirit could overshadow Mary without conflict.

b. Jesus is still called the only begotten of the Father without contradiction.

3. Mormons misuse texts concerning Christ's mission.

---

[93]*Doctrines of Salvation,* 1:33.

[94]*Journal of Discourses,* 6:4.

    a. John 1:14 (1:18; 3:16) uses "only begotten" to describe Jesus.

       (1) The Greek New Testament word is *monogenes,* meaning the "unique one" or "one of a kind." Hence, we have the NIV translation "the One and Only" Son.

       (2) The term emphasizes Christ's uniqueness; it has nothing to do with being begotten in the natural sense.

    b. John 2:1–11 is not an account of one of Jesus' weddings.

       (1) Verse 2 says Jesus and his disciples were "invited" to the wedding, so it could not have been his wedding.

       (2) Also, Jesus was of the same status as his disciples; they were all invited.

    c. Isaiah 53:10 is a messianic prophecy that speaks of the Messiah's death and resurrection.

       (1) The text reads, "Yet it was the LORD's will to crush him, and cause him to suffer, and though the LORD makes his life a guilt offering, he will see his offspring and prolong his days, and the will of the LORD will prosper in his hand."

       (2) The death of the Messiah precedes the seed and the prolonging of days. This prolonging of days is understood as the resurrection of Jesus. The offspring or seed are the believers after his resurrection.

D. The Biblical Doctrine on Jesus' Life and Exaltation

  1. Scripture teaches the virgin birth of Jesus Christ.

    a. Matthew 1:18—Mary was pregnant "before" she and Joseph came together; Mary's virginity was an important point for Matthew.

    b. Matthew 1:20—The angel appeared to Joseph telling him that the child was conceived by the Holy Spirit.

    c. Matthew 1:23—Matthew used the Greek word *parthenos* for "virgin," which means a young woman who has never had sexual intercourse.[95]

    d. Matthew 1:25—Joseph continued to abstain from union with Mary until Jesus was born.

    e. Luke 1:34—When Gabriel told Mary she would bear Jesus she asked how it could be, since she was a virgin.

    f. Luke 1:35–37—Gabriel told Mary that the Holy Spirit would bring about the miracle.

  2. Jesus' mission was to atone for the world's sins.

    a. Jesus' purpose was known in prophecy.

       (1) He will be God with humanity (Isa. 7:14; 9:6).

---

[95]Dr. William White, Jr. states, "At no point in the NT is the term *parthenos* ever used apart from virgins" (*Zondervan Pictorial Encyclopedia of the Bible*, 5:886).

       (2) He will be a Prophet, Priest, and King (Deut. 18:15; Ps. 110:4; Isa. 9:7).

       (3) He will preach the gospel to the poor and deliverance to the captives (Isa. 61:1).

       (4) He will be rejected by his people and crucified for the sins of the world (Isa. 53:3–10).

       (5) He will rise victorious over death and ascend to heaven (Ps. 16:10; 68:18).

  b. Jesus' purpose was known at his conception.

       (1) He will save people from their sins (Matt. 1:21).

       (2) He will rule as king (Luke 1:32–33).

  c. Jesus' purpose was known at his birth.

       (1) He is Christ the Lord (Luke 1:33).

       (2) He is the salvation of God (Luke 1:31).

  d. Jesus' purpose was known from his baptism.

       (1) He is the Lamb of God who takes away the sin of the world (John 1:29).

       (2) He will separate the chaff from the wheat (Matt. 3:12).

  e. Jesus knew his own purpose.

       (1) He came to give his life as a ransom for many (Mark 10:45).

       (2) He came to give abundant life (John 10:10).

       (3) He came to have victory over the grave (1 Cor. 15:55–57).

       (4) He came as the only way to heaven (John 10:1–8).

VI. The Holy Spirit

A. *The Mormon View of the Holy Ghost and Holy Spirit Briefly Stated*

  1. Early Mormonism differentiated the Holy Ghost from the Holy Spirit.

  2. The distinction is less prevalent today.[96]

  3. There are distinctions between the Holy Ghost and the Holy Spirit.

    a. The Holy Ghost

       (1) Is a spirit-child, born of Heavenly Parents, and has the shape of a man

       (2) Can only be in one location at a time

       (3) Is one of three Gods in the Godhead

---

[96]In some modern Mormon writings the distinction between the Holy Ghost and Holy Spirit still exists, but the terms are becoming interchangeable.

    b. The Holy Spirit

        (1) Is a divine eminence or influence

        (2) Can be felt by Mormons universally

        (3) Bears witness to the truths of Mormonism

B. *Arguments Mormons Use to Support Their View of the Holy Ghost and Holy Spirit*

1. Joseph Fielding Smith distinguished between the Holy Ghost and Holy Spirit. "The Holy Ghost should not be confused with the Spirit which fills the immensity of space and which is everywhere present. This other Spirit is impersonal and has no size, nor dimension; it proceeds forth from the presence of the Father and the Son and is in all things. We should speak of the Holy Ghost as a personage as 'he' and this other Spirit as 'it.'"[97]

2. The Holy Ghost is a male offspring of the Father. As Joseph F. McConkie wrote, "The Holy Ghost is a spirit man, a spirit son of God the Father.... a personage of spirit separate and distinct from both the Father and the Son.... the third member of the Eternal Godhead."[98]

3. The Holy Ghost has limitations. Apostle LeGrand Richards taught that the Holy Ghost is a personage of spirit in the form of man (see 1 Nephi 11:11) and hence confined in his personage to a limited space.[99]

4. The Holy Spirit is a divine influence.

    a. President Joseph F. Smith wrote, "The Holy Spirit ... is the influence of Deity, the light of Christ, or of Truth, which proceeds forth from the presence of God to fill the immensity of space, and to quicken the understanding of men."[100]

    b. Joseph Smith said: "Do the Father and Son possess the same mind?... What is this mind? The Holy Spirit."[101]

5. Mormons use Scripture to support their view of the Holy Ghost and Holy Spirit.

    a. Luke 3:22—The Holy Ghost descended in bodily shape as a dove, showing that the Holy Ghost has shape and is not omnipresent.

    b. John 15:26—The Holy Spirit proceeds from the Father, which shows that the spirit is an influence.

---

[97]*Doctrines of Salvation,* 1:50.

[98]Ludlow, *Encyclopedia of Mormonism,* 2:649.

[99]LeGrand Richards, *A Marvelous Work and a Wonder* (Salt Lake City: Deseret Book Co., 1973), 117.

[100]Joseph E. Smith, *Improvement Era* (Salt Lake City: The Church of Jesus Christ of Latter-day Saints), 389.

[101]*Lectures on Faith* (Salt Lake City: N. B. Lundwall, n.d.), 25. Note: The *Lectures on Faith* were sermons on theology delivered by Joseph Smith in 1834 at the School of the Prophets in Kirtland, Ohio. They were originally published with the Doctrine and Covenants, 1835 edition, but later removed. Smith intended the lectures to be theology for the church.

C. Refutation of Arguments Mormons Use to Support Their Position on the Holy Ghost and Holy Spirit

1. Joseph Smith's distinction between the Holy Ghost and Holy Spirit reveals his lack of biblical knowledge because both terms are translated from the same Greek words *pneuma hagion*.

   a. The words "Holy Ghost" are archaic Elizabethan English for "Holy Spirit."

      (1) "Ghost" was also a common reference for a person's spirit.

      (2) In English, "ghost" comes from the German *Geist*, meaning "spirit."

   b. A simple comparison of the accounts of Jesus' baptism (KJV) illustrates how the two terms are perfectly interchangeable.

      (1) Matthew uses "Spirit of God" (3:16).

      (2) Mark uses "Spirit" (1:10).

      (3) Luke uses "Holy Ghost" (3:22).

      (4) John uses "Spirit" (1:32).

2. Mormons do not correctly handle the biblical texts concerning the Holy Spirit.

   a. Luke 3:22 does not demonstrate that the Holy Ghost has a finite shape, but that the Holy Spirit made himself visible, the same as any theophany (a visible and audible manifestation of God) in Scripture.

   b. John 15:26 does not depersonalize the Holy Spirit just because he proceeds from the Father; if that were the case, Jesus would not be a person either, since he proceeded from the Father (8:42).

D. The Biblical Doctrine of the Holy Spirit

1. The Holy Spirit is a person (i.e., he has that which characterizes personhood).

   a. Knowledge (1 Cor. 2:10–11)

   b. Emotion (Eph. 4:30)

   c. Love (Rom. 15:30)

   d. Will (1 Cor. 12:11)

   e. Mind (Rom. 8:27)

2. The Holy Spirit is God (2 Sam. 23:2–3; Acts 5:1–4; 1 Cor. 6:19–20).

   a. The Holy Spirit is omnipresent (Ps. 139:7–10).

   b. The Holy Spirit is omnipotent (Luke 1:35–37).

   c. The Holy Spirit is omniscient (Isa. 40:13).

   d. The Holy Spirit is eternal (Heb. 9:14).

   e. Compare Psalm 95:7–11 with Hebrews 3:7–19; Isaiah 6:8–10 with Acts 28:25–27; Jeremiah 31:33–34 with Hebrews 10:15–16.

VII. Humanity

A. *The Mormon View of Humanity Briefly Stated*

1. Human beings preexisted as organized intelligences.

2. These intelligences were born of Heavenly Parents and are gods in an embryonic state.

3. Part of their progression to godhood includes a probationary period on earth.

4. There was a great war in heaven that divided the children of God into two camps.

   a. One-third followed Lucifer and two-thirds followed Jesus in battle.

   b. Of the two-thirds who followed Jesus, one-third were less valiant than the other, so they received black skin when they came to earth (thus explaining the Negro race).

5. Adam transgressed but did not sin.

6. Adam's transgression is not passed on to the human race; each person is responsible only for his or her own sins.

7. The ultimate goal of humanity is to become a perfected god.

B. *Arguments Mormons Use to Support Their View of Humanity*

1. All humanity, including Jesus, has forgotten their preexistence as embryonic gods.[102]

   a. Presidency member John Taylor said, "In another point of view, we look at him [humankind] as emanating from the Gods—as a God in embryo—as an eternal being who had an existence before he came here."[103]

   b. Brigham Young said, "The intelligence we possess is from our Father and our God. Every attribute that is in His character is in His children in embryo."[104]

2. The various human races are due to a preexistent war in heaven.

   a. The war began because Lucifer's plan of salvation was rejected. "In this great rebellion in heaven, Lucifer, or Satan, a son of the morning, and one-third of the hosts thereof were cast out into the earth because Lucifer sought to destroy the free agency of man and one-third of the spirits sided with him. He sought the throne of God, and put forth his plan in boldness in that great council, de-

---

[102]According to Joseph Fielding Smith, human beings are predetermined to forget their preexistence when they arrive on earth: "Without doubt, Jesus came into the world subject to the same condition as was required of each of us—he forgot everything, and he had to grow from grace to grace. His forgetting, or having his former knowledge taken away, would be requisite just as it is in the case of each of us, to complete the present temporal existence" (*Doctrines of Salvation*, 1:32).

[103]*Journal of Discourses*, 8:1.

[104]*Journal of Discourses*, 12:105.

claring that he would save all, that not one soul should be lost, provided God would give him the glory and the honor. When his plan was rejected for a better one, he rebelled."[105]

b. Jesus organized the other angels in battle. "There were no neutrals in the war in heaven. All took sides either with Christ or with Satan."[106]

c. The less valiant angels were cursed to become Negroes on earth.

(1) "We naturally conclude that others among the two-thirds did not show the loyalty to their Redeemer that they should. That the Negro race, for instance, have [sic] been placed under restrictions because of their attitude in the world of spirits, few will doubt."[107]

(2) "Every man had his agency there, and men receive rewards here based upon their actions there, just as they will receive rewards hereafter for deeds done in the body. The Negro, evidently, is receiving the reward he merits."[108]

3. At one time Brigham Young taught that Adam was God, even the father of Jesus Christ.[109]

a. Brigham Young espoused this doctrine in 1852. "Now hear it, O inhabitants of the earth, Jew and Gentile, Saints and Sinners! When our father Adam came into the garden of Eden, he came into it with a celestial body, and brought Eve, one of his wives, with him. He helped to make and organize this world. He is Michael, the Archangel, the Ancient of Days! about whom holy men have written and spoken—He is our Father and our God, and the only God with whom we have to do. When the Virgin Mary conceived the child Jesus, the Father had begotten him in his own likeness. He was not begotten by the Holy Ghost. And who is the Father? He is the first of the human family; and when he took a tabernacle, it was begotten by his father in heaven, after the same manner as the tabernacles of Cain [and] Abel. . . ."[110]

b. Twenty-one years later Young was still teaching the Adam-God doctrine. "How much unbelief exists in the minds of the Latter-day Saints in regard to one particular doctrine which I revealed to

---

[105]Smith, *Doctrines of Salvation,* 1:64.

[106]Smith, *Doctrines of Salvation,* 1:65.

[107]Joseph Fielding Smith, *The Way to Perfection* (Salt Lake City, Deseret Book Co., 1975), 43.

[108]Smith, *Doctrines of Salvation,* 1:65–66.

[109]The Adam-god doctrine has been one of the primary points of separation between Mormonism and Christianity since the mid-1800s. Although the Mormon Church today repudiates the doctrine, it cannot deny the historical evidence of its permeation in nineteenth-century Mormonism (cf. *Journal of Discourses,* 1:50–51; 4:271; 5:331; *Millennial Star,* 15:769, 801, 825; 16:482, 534; 17:195; *Deseret News,* 18 June, 1873, 308). The only splinter groups of Mormonism that still believe this doctrine are Fundamentalist Mormons.

[110]*Journal of Discourses,* 1:50.

them, and which God revealed to me—namely that Adam is our father and God. Our Father Adam helped to make this earth, it was created expressly for him, and after it was made he and his companions came here. He brought one of his wives with him, and she was called Eve."[111]

4. When Adam transgressed, he did not sin, but rather "fell upward."

    a. Joseph Fielding Smith said, "I never speak of the part Eve took in this fall as a sin, nor do I accuse Adam of a sin. It is true, the Lord warned Adam and Eve that to partake of the fruit they would transgress a law, and this happened. But it is not always a sin to transgress a law ... that is, his transgression was in accordance with law."[112]

    b. Sterling Sill, assistant to the apostles, explained that Adam fell "but he fell in the right direction. He fell toward the goal. Adam fell, but he fell upward."[113]

5. Adam's guilt did not pass on to the human race. "We believe that all men will be punished for their own sins, and not for Adam's transgression."[114]

6. A man's potential destiny is to become a god and his wife a goddess.[115]

    a. Humanity is designed to have an earth and populate it. According to Heber C. Kimball, "When you have learned to become obedient to the Father that dwells upon this earth, to the Father and God of this earth, and obedient to the messengers He sends—when you have done all that, remember you are not going to leave this earth.

---

[111]*Deseret News*, 18 June 1873, 308.

[112]Smith, *Doctrines of Salvation*, 1:114.

[113]*Deseret News*, 31 July 1965, Church Section, 7.

[114]Pearl of Great Price, Articles of Faith, 2.

[115]The Eastern Orthodox Church has a doctrine called "deification," which teaches that God's communicable attributes are imparted to humanity in the resurrection. This is not a foreign concept to students of theology. Mormon apologists, however, have distorted Orthodox writings concerning humanity becoming like God and construed them to be equal with the Latter-day Saint view of godhood. Not only does this do violence to the context of the Orthodox doctrine of deification, it falsely equivocates terms that are mutually contradictory. Orthodoxy and the early church fathers who made statements about the human potential to acquire attributes of God always made a clear distinction on three points: (1) there is but one true God; humanity is forever distinct from the nature of God; (2) God's communicable attributes—love, mercy, holiness, and the like—have reference to man's glorification in the resurrection; (3) God's incommunicable attributes (eternality, omniscience, omnipresence, omnipotence, immutability, transcendence, and self-existence) are not given to humanity in the resurrection. There is therefore a qualitative difference between what Orthodoxy calls "deification" and what Mormons call "godhood."

    The differences between deification and Mormonism were debated between a Mormon apologetic panel and a Christian apologetic panel at Biola University. See Van Hale, Bill Forrest, Bob Passantino, and Kurt Van Gorden, *The Christian and Mormon Debates on Theology* (Orange, Calif.: Jude 3 Missions, 1991), available through Jude 3 Missions, P. O. Box 1901, Orange, CA 92668. For a good understanding of the Orthodox view see David N. Bell, *A Cloud of Witnesses* (Kalamazoo, Mich.: Cistercian Publications, 1989); Daniel B. Clendenin, "Partakers of Divinity: The Orthodox Doctrine of Theosis," *Journal of the Evangelical Theological Society* 37, no. 3 (September 1994): 365–79.

You will never leave it until you become qualified, and capable, and capacitated to become a father of an earth yourselves."[116]

b. Children begin their existence as gods in embryo, and endlessly repeat the cycle. As Joseph Fielding Smith explains, "The Father has promised us that through our faithfulness we shall be blessed with the fullness of his kingdom. In other words we will have the privilege of becoming like him. To become like him we must have all the powers of godhood; thus a man and his wife when glorified will have spirit children who eventually will go on an earth like this one we are on and pass through the same kind of experiences, being subject to mortal conditions, and if faithful, then they also will receive the fullness of exaltation and partake of the same blessings. There is no end to this development; it will go on forever."[117]

7. Mormons use Scripture (KJV) to support their view of humanity.

   a. Exodus 7:1—The Lord said he had made Moses "a god" to Pharaoh.

   b. Psalm 82:1, 6—These verses say that all people are the offspring of God, and as his children, they are gods.

   c. Ecclesiastes 12:7—Since "the spirit shall return unto God who gave it," this means that people preexisted with God and will return to him.

   d. Jeremiah 1:5—Since God knew Jeremiah before he was born, Jeremiah must have preexisted in heaven before his birth.

   e. Matthew 5:48—God expects us to become gods like him ("perfect"), which is the road to personal perfection.

   f. John 10:34—Jesus proclaimed that people can become gods when he said to the Jews "Is it not written in your law, I said, Ye are gods?"

   g. Romans 8:16–17—Being the children of God and joint heirs with Christ, people will become gods like Christ before them.

   h. Revelation 1:6 (5:10)—These verses speak of "kings and priests" (KJV), which means that, in the exaltation, people will become gods.

C. *Refutation of Arguments Mormons Use to Support Their View of Humanity*

   1. The preexistence of humanity is illogical and unscriptural.

      a. When Brigham Young said that man existed first in the spiritual realm and then in the natural realm, he reversed Paul in 1 Corinthians 15:46: "That was not first which is spiritual, but that which is natural; and afterward that which is spiritual" (KJV).

---

[116]*Journal of Discourses*, 1:356.
[117]*Doctrines of Salvation*, 2:48.

    b. If human beings are first spiritual, we run into the logical absurdity of the infinite regression of spiritual entities preceding physical entities (see section II.C.3 above).

        (1) Once a god and his goddess-wife procreate spirit-children in heaven (a spiritual entity—an organized intelligence), then these children are sent to an earth in physical bodies for their probationary period and have the opportunity to progress to godhood also.

        (2) When we look backward at this line of gods who were once men and preexisted as spiritual entities, there is no end to the line, no beginning.

        (3) A line of succession that has no beginning cannot exist since it is always relying upon a former existence; hence there must have been a beginning to such a succession.

        (4) If such a succession had a beginning, then whatever lies beyond the beginning is greater than the succession, since it preceded the succession and did not rely on the succession for its existence.

        (5) Since Mormonism does not provide for a God who exists beyond this cycle, the succession of preexistent spirits who become gods falls into the logical absurdity of infinite regression.

2. The racism inherent in the Mormon view of human preexistence and earthly dwelling is biblically indefensible.

    a. Since there was no human preexistence (see C.1. above), black people could not have been cursed for being "lesser-valiant" in a preexistent war in heaven.

    b. Scripture indicates that a racial curse is foreign to God's design for man.

        (1) Acts 10:34–35—"God does not show favoritism but accepts men from every nation who fear him and do what is right."

        (2) Galatians 2:6—"God does not judge by external appearance."

        (3) Galatians 3:28—"There is neither Jew nor Greek, slave nor free, male nor female, for you are all one in Christ Jesus."

3. Mormons misuse Scripture to support their view of humanity.

    a. Exodus 7:1 does not say that Moses is a god or can become a god; Moses was certainly not worthy of worship or adoration, but was only God's vessel before Pharaoh.

    b. Psalm 82:1 and 6 speak about the judges of Israel who were not judging fairly.

        (1) They were called "gods" because the Word of God was spoken through them.

        (2) They were poor judges, however, and needed judgment themselves (see vv. 2–3).

    (3) They were still men (v. 7), and their nature would not change in any respect—their death would prove it.

    (4) The contrast between the true God and these judges called gods (v. 1) shows that they still answer to the one and true God, and therefore are not gods at all.

  c. Ecclesiastes 12:7 does not show that people preexisted with God before they were born on earth.

    (1) The proper reading of this verse must include two aspects of humanity, dust and spirit. Dust is used figuratively for the body (Gen. 2:7; 3:19; Ps. 104:29). Spirit is used of man's spirit (James 2:26).

    (2) The word "return," used of both the body and spirit, merely shows that the material nature of human beings decays and goes back to the earth (dust) while the immaterial nature goes to God. It no more speaks of the preexistence of the soul than it does the individual preexistence of the body (dust). The spirit returns to God to await judgment, not because each individual began there. The original spirit of humanity was given by God, just as God gave Adam a body of dust.

  d. Jeremiah 1:5 speaks of God's foreknowledge, not Jeremiah's preexistence.

    (1) The emphasis is upon what God knows, not what Jeremiah is. Jeremiah's existence is not the criterion for God's language, since God knows all things.

    (2) Romans 4:17 tells us that God, who knows all things, speaks of things that do not exist as though they do.

    (3) Psalm 139:16 also enlightens us about how God ordains life for one who does not yet exist: "Your eyes saw my unformed body. All the days ordained for me were written in your book before one of them came to be."

  e. Matthew 5:48 does not command human perfectionism and progression to godhood.

    (1) The context of this verse (vv. 43–48) is the fact that God shows no partiality toward the just and the unjust in their daily living. Just as God gives sunlight to both the evil and the good and rain to the just and the unjust, Christians are to love both the just and the unjust.

    (2) The word "therefore" (v. 48) necessarily refers back to the context of unconditional love. Be "perfect" in your love as your Father is perfect in his love. Be perfect in your impartiality as your Father is perfect in his impartiality. This we are to strive for as Christians, knowing that ultimate perfection awaits us in the resurrection.

f. In John 10:34, Jesus quotes Psalm 82:6 (see 3.b. above), contrasting his true deity with those who can make no claim to deity.

(1) The judges of the Old Testament were "called" gods (v. 35). The fact that they were "called" gods indicates they are not really gods at all. They were called gods because the word of God came to them to judge human affairs. The expression "called God" is never used of Christ for he *is* God.

(2) Jesus gives the contrast, saying, "What about the one whom the Father set apart as his very own and sent into the world? Why then do you accuse me of blasphemy because I said, 'I am God's Son'?" (v. 36). Jesus speaks of himself as "the one" who was set apart and sent, whereas the so-called gods were neither. Therefore, Jesus has the right to claim he is the Son of God— which is tantamount to saying he is God (v. 33)—effectively showing that he is truly God and that those who were called gods were not worthy of the title.

g. Although Romans 8:16–17 speaks of Christians being children of God and co-heirs with Christ, this does not mean we will obtain a divine nature.

(1) Christians are children of God by virtue of adoption (see NIV note at v. 15), which means we are not God's children by nature, but must be "adopted" into his family (see also Rom. 8:23; 9:4; Eph. 1:5).

(2) One could reasonably be a joint-heir without changing his or her nature. Using the example of the sexes, if one is an heir of a fortune, it has nothing to do with the *nature* of his or her sex; he or she can still be an heir. Just because a woman may leave a fortune to a male relative, the man's nature does not change because he becomes an heir, likewise, becoming a joint-heir with Christ does not alter our nature into godhood.

h. Revelation 1:6 (see also 5:10) is best translated as "made us to be a kingdom and priests" (NIV).

(1) In Christ's kingdom Christians will be his subjects for eternity.

(2) This does not make us gods.

(3) The priesthood of believers is outlined in 1 Peter 2:5, 9; we shall be priests within his kingdom.

D. The Biblical Doctrine of Humanity

1. Humanity is a direct creation of God, beginning with Adam and Eve.

a. Both man and woman are made in the image and likeness of God (Gen. 1:27).

(1) This image and likeness of God is spiritual, since both genders share it equally.

        (2) The physical distinction of the sexes prevents the image and likeness of God from being physical (Gen. 2:7, 21–22).

    b. God blessed man and woman and commanded them to rule over the earth (Gen. 1:28).

  2. God gave men and women rationality, consciousness, and moral freedom.

    a. Adam and Eve chose to break God's commandments and thus sin entered the world (Gen. 3).

    b. In response to their sin God cursed humanity and the earth (Gen. 3:14–19).

  3. Through Adam, sin was passed on to all the human race.

    a. All people are sinful from birth (Rom. 5:12; Ps. 51:5).

    b. By nature human beings are children of "wrath" (Eph. 2:3), with no hope of saving themselves (Eph. 2:12).

    c. People are without excuse before God (Rom. 1:18–20) and stand in unrighteousness and guilt (Rom. 3:19; Gal. 3:22).

    d. The result of sin is death (Ezek. 18:20; Rom. 6:23).

  4. Human nature is both material and immaterial, body and soul.

    a. Upon death the body is separated from the spirit (Eccl. 12:1–7; James 2:26).

    b. The spirit shall be reunited with the body in the resurrection.

VIII. The Atonement of Christ and Salvation

A. *The Mormon View of Christ's Atonement and Salvation Briefly Stated*

  1. There are two effects of Christ's atonement.

    a. All humankind will be resurrected.

    b. It sets one on the road to exaltation.

  2. The atonement of Christ took place in the garden of Gethsemane where he sweat great drops of blood.

  3. The purpose of the atonement: Christ's atonement was only for Adam's transgression.

  4. Salvation: Individual salvation begins with the atonement, but is completed through human works.

    a. Some sins cannot be covered by Christ's atonement; people must atone for these sins themselves.

    b. Baptism is a necessary human work and can be applied, by proxy, to the deceased.

  5. There are three degrees of heaven.

    a. The three levels are Telestial, Terrestrial, and Celestial.

    b. People go to one level or the other according to their works.

61

B. Arguments Mormons Use to Support Their View of Christ's Atonement and Salvation

1. Twofold Application of the Atonement and Salvation

   a. *General* salvation

     Joseph Fielding Smith explained: "Every soul born upon the face of this earth shall come forth in the resurrection, either of the just or of the unjust, for the resurrection shall be universal, and that, too, through the great atonement which was made by the Savior of the world."[118]

   b. *Specific* salvation

     McConkie said, "Because there was such an atonement, man can have faith, perform the works of righteousness, endure to the end, and 'work out [his] own salvation with fear and trembling' (Phil. 2:12)."[119]

2. Only for Adam's Transgressions

   a. Christ's atonement was for Adam's transgression only.

   b. Apostle LeGrand Richards said, "Jesus Christ redeemed all from the fall; he paid the price; he offered himself as a ransom; he atoned for Adam's sin, leaving us responsible only for our own sins."[120]

   c. The second Article of Faith states, "We believe that men will be punished for their own sins, and not for Adam's transgression."[121]

3. Christ's atonement was accomplished in the garden of Gethsemane. "And then there is Gethsemane, the garden of the olive press, where he sweat great drops of blood from every pore, so great was his suffering and so intense his anguish as he took upon himself the sins of all men on conditions of repentance."[122]

4. The Necessity of Works

   a. Individual salvation necessitates works in addition to Christ's atonement.

   b. Those who die before eight years of age are exempt from works and automatically inherit the celestial kingdom (Doctrine and Covenants 137:10).

   c. The necessity of works is shown in the first principles of the gospel, outlined in the fourth Article of Faith: "We believe that the first principles and ordinances of the Gospel are: first, Faith in the Lord Jesus Christ; second, Repentance; third, Baptism by immersion for the remission of sins; fourth, Laying on of hands for the gift of the Holy Ghost."

[118]Smith, *Doctrines of Salvation,* 1:160.

[119]McConkie, *A New Witness for the Articles of Faith,* (Salt Lake City: Deseret Book Co., 1985), 150.

[120]Richards, *A Marvelous Work and a Wonder,* 98.

[121]Articles of Faith 2.

[122]Bruce R. McConkie, *The Mortal Messiah* (Salt Lake City: Deseret Book Co., 1979), 4:229.

d. Additional works that are necessary may include temple work, mission work, fulfilling a church position, tithing, or the covenants, as summarized by Joseph F. Smith: "Among the covenants are these, that they will cease from sin and from all unrighteousness; that they will work righteousness in their lives; that they will abstain from the use of intoxicants, from the use of strong drinks of every description, from the use of tobacco, from every vile thing, and from extremes in every phase of life; that they will not take the name of God in vain; that they will not bear false witness against their neighbor; that they will seek to love their neighbors as themselves; to carry out the golden rule of the Lord, do unto others as they would that others should do unto them. These principles are involved in the covenants that the people have made in the Church of Jesus Christ of Latter-day Saints.... Those who have entered into the covenant of the gospel will keep the commandments of the Lord, will obey the dictates of the Spirit of the Lord unto them, will work righteousness in the earth, and will go right on in the path that Almighty God has marked out for them to pursue, fulfilling and accomplishing his will and his purposes concerning them in the latter day."[123]

e. Ultimate salvation cannot be obtained without confessing Joseph Smith as a prophet. As Brigham Young preached, "The time was when the test of a Christian was his confession of Christ. This is no test to this generation, for all men of the Christian world confess that Jesus Christ has come in the flesh. This generation, however, is not left without a test. I have taught for thirty years, and still teach, that he that believeth in his heart and confesseth with his mouth that Jesus is the Christ and that Joseph Smith is his Prophet to this generation, is of God; and he that confesseth not that Jesus has come in the flesh and sent Joseph Smith with the fullness of the Gospel to this generation, is not of God, but is anti-christ."[124]

f. Some sins cannot be covered by Christ's atonement, so people must atone themselves. According to Brigham Young, "There is not a man or woman, who violates the covenants made with their God, that will not be required to pay the debt. The blood of Christ will never wipe that out, your own blood must atone for it; and the judgments of the Almighty will come, sooner or later, and every man and woman will have to atone for breaking their covenants."[125]

g. Those in hell can eventually atone for their sins.

Brigham Young taught, "He will be damned; in hell he will lift up his eyes, being in torment, until he has paid the uttermost

---

[123]Smith, *Gospel Doctrine,* 107.
[124]*Journal of Discourses,* 9:312.
[125]*Journal of Discourses,* 3:247.

farthing, and made a full atonement for his sins. It is this very class of men, though not all of them, who have set up such a howl against the doctrine of polygamy."[126]

5. The Three Degrees of Heaven[127]

a. The *telestial* kingdom

"Most of the adult people who have lived from the day of Adam to the present time will go to the telestial kingdom ... for all such have lived a telestial law. 'And they shall be servants of the Most High; but where God and Christ dwell they cannot come, worlds without end.' (D & C 76:112)."[128]

b. The *terrestrial* kingdom

"To the terrestrial kingdom will go: 1. Accountable persons who die without law ... ; 2. Those who reject the gospel in this life and who reverse their course and accept it in the spirit world; 3. Honorable men of the earth who are blinded by the craftiness of men and who therefore do not accept and live the gospel law; and 4. Members of The Church of Jesus Christ of Latter-day Saints who have testimonies of Christ and the divinity of the great latter-day work and who are not valiant, but who are instead lukewarm in their devotion to the Church and to righteousness (D & C 76:71–80)."[129]

c. The *celestial* kingdom

"An inheritance in this glorious kingdom is gained by complete obedience to gospel or celestial law. (D & C 88:16–32). By entering the gate of repentance and baptism candidates find themselves on the strait and narrow path leading to the celestial kingdom. By devotion and faithfulness, by enduring to the end in righteousness and obedience, it is then possible to merit a celestial reward. (2 Ne. 31:17–21.)"[130]

(1) Temple marriage is required for the celestial kingdom. "In the same sense that baptism starts a person out toward an entrance into the celestial world, so celestial marriage puts a couple on the path leading to an exaltation in the highest heaven of that world. (D & C 131:1–4; 132.)"[131]

(2) Obedience to moral laws is also a condition of entrance. That law by obedience to which men gain an inheritance in the

---

[126]*Journal of Discourses,* 11:268.

[127]Mormon theologians give relatively little discussion of just what these three heavens are. Instead, they talk a great deal about how one qualifies for each level. From the few references given, it appears that the levels of heaven correspond to "worlds, different departments, or mansions," varying in degree of glory (*Journal of Discourses,* 1:312; cf. Joseph Fielding Smith, *Doctrines of Salvation,* 1:72).

[128]McConkie, *Mormon Doctrine,* 778.

[129]McConkie, *Mormon Doctrine,* 784.

[130]McConkie, *Mormon Doctrine,* 116.

[131]McConkie, *Mormon Doctrine,* 116.

kingdom of God in eternity is called celestial law. It is the law of the gospel, the law of Christ, and it qualifies men for admission to the celestial kingdom because in and through it men are 'sanctified by the reception of the Holy Ghost,' thus becoming clean, pure, and spotless. (3 Ne. 27:19–21.)"[132]

6. Mormons as Saviors of Other Men

   a. The Doctrine and Covenants 103:9 says, "For they were set to be a light unto the world, and to be the saviors of men."

   b. Through baptism for the dead they become saviors of men.

   According to Joseph Fielding Smith, "Through it we become saviors on Mount Zion, and may save multitudes of our kin."[133]

   c. This explains Mormons' interest in genealogy.

   Brigham Young called Mormons "Saviors on Mount Zion," saying, "We have a work to do just as important in its sphere as the Savior's work was in its sphere. Our fathers cannot be made perfect without us; we cannot be made perfect without them. They have done their work and now sleep. We are now called upon to do ours; which is to be the greatest work man ever performed on the earth. Millions of our fellow creatures who have lived upon the earth and died without a knowledge of the Gospel must be officiated for in order that they may inherit eternal life (that is, all that would have received the Gospel)."[134]

7. Scriptures Mormons Use to Support Their View (KJV)

   a. Obadiah 21—This verse speaks of men as saviors: "Saviours shall come up on mount Zion to judge the mount of Esau; and the kingdom shall be the LORD's."

   b. Mark 16:16—The statement "He that believeth and is baptized shall be saved" shows that baptism is essential to salvation.

   c. John 3:5—When Jesus said you must be "born of water" he meant baptism, thus showing that it is essential to salvation.

   d. 1 Corinthians 15:29—"Else what shall they do which are baptized for the dead, if the dead rise not at all? why are they then baptized for the dead?"

   e. 1 Corinthians 15:40–41—The various kingdoms of heaven are described as celestial, terrestrial, and glories.

   f. 2 Corinthians 12:2—The words "third heaven" confirm the concept of three kingdoms.

   g. Philippians 2:12—The command to "work out your own salvation with fear and trembling" illustrates that works are a vital part of one's salvation.

---

[132]McConkie, *Mormon Doctrine*, 117.

[133]*Doctrines of Salvation*, 1:268.

[134]*Journal of Discourses*, 18:213.

h. James 2:26—Works are a part of one's salvation, since "faith without works is dead."

i. 1 Peter 3:19—This verse teaches that Christ preached to the dead. "By which also he [Christ] went and preached unto the spirits in prison."

j. 1 Peter 4:6—Peter taught that Christ offered salvation to the dead: "For this cause was the gospel preached also to them that are dead, that they might be judged according to men in the flesh, but live according to God in the spirit."

C. Refutation of Mormon Arguments on Christ's Atonement and Salvation

1. The alleged sinlessness of those under eight years of age is problematic.

   a. If sin and guilt is not passed on to the human race through Adam, and a person under age eight is innocent, then the person can be said to be innocent, sinless, pure and guilt-free.

   b. Why, then, do the Latter-day Saints baptize eight-year-olds for remission of sins if there are no sins for which they need remission?

   c. If the subject is already pure, then he does not become better through the baptism since there is theoretically nothing in him to condemn him.

   d. Therefore, the baptism is valueless; it remits nothing since nothing was there to remit.

2. In Christianity, works are not the means of salvation or glorification.

   a. James 2:26

      (1) It is true that James said "faith without works is dead," but James never prescribes works as the way of salvation.

      (2) James teaches faith as the way and works as the *testimony* of saving faith.

      (3) James speaks first of faith in Jesus Christ (2:1) and then brings in the discussion about faith and works throughout chapter 2.

   b. Titus 2:5

      When faith and works are mentioned in connection with the Christian life, faith always precedes the works and works always are the evidence of faith.

   c. Ephesians 2:8–10

      Works cannot produce nor help faith, but they become the testimony to the outside world of the genuineness of one's faith.

3. The Mormon doctrine of baptism for the dead presents a problem for how to apply it to the dead person.

   a. If someone were to be baptized for a dead person there is no way to know whether the person actually "received" the gospel message in the "spirit world."

  b. If the dead person baptized by proxy has the choice of receiving or rejecting the gospel message in the spirit world, it is be probable that some spirits would reject the message, which then means the baptism would be invalid.

  c. The living person being baptized for the dead has no way of knowing whether the message was received by the dead person, so if he baptizes for the dead "just in case" the message is received, the act is a mere charade of what may or may not be true.

4. It is impossible to baptize every past living person.

  a. Entire nations and civilizations have developed and died out without any record, minus a few bones and artifacts.

   (1) If fairness was the object of baptism for the dead, then Mormons escape nothing and find themselves within the same "trap" of which they accuse Christians.

   (2) One needs only to ask the Mormon about the hundreds of thousands of lives that will never and can never be accounted for because no evidence remains for their existence. If we find a few arrowheads and pottery fragments in a digging, it tells us nothing about how many people lived in the area, when they lived, or what their names were. Therefore, it is impossible to baptize people on behalf of these people of the past, since nothing is known of them. Multiply this example by every island and continent on the earth and we see the enormous problem created by Mormon baptism for the dead.

   (3) Baptism for the dead, then, does not address a concern for "fairness" to those who died without hearing the gospel.

  b. Scripture condemns keeping endless genealogies.

   (1) 1 Timothy 1:4—Genealogies "promote controversies rather than God's work—which is by faith."

   (2) Titus 3:9—Genealogies are to be avoided "because these are unprofitable and useless."

5. The Mormon concept of three heavens is unbiblical (for a refutation of this see section X.C.2. below, which deals with the Mormon view of the end times).

6. Mormons misinterpret Scripture in attempting to prove their doctrine of atonement and salvation.

  a. The word "saviours" (KJV) in Obadiah 21 is better translated "deliverers" (NIV).

   (1) The context preceding this verse speaks of war and deliverance from nations, which establishes the meaning of the Hebrew word *moshiim* as "deliverers."

   (2) The text does not introduce even a remote concept of human saviors of people's souls.

b. Mark 16:16 does teach that baptized believers are saved.

(1) All believers who are also baptized will be saved; however, un-baptized believers are not unsaved, as Mormons attempt to force upon it.

(2) The next clause, "whoever does not believe will be con-demned," supports the view that belief in Christ saves, and not baptism; it does not say "he that is unbaptized is damned."

c. In John 3:5 Jesus was speaking to Nicodemus about being "born again," literally, "born from above" (NIV note for v. 3).

(1) The way of salvation through faith in Jesus Christ is given in verses 15 and 16.

(2) The context of chapter three leaves no doubt that belief in Jesus is the only way of eternal life. Even though historically there have been various understandings of what the word "water" means in chapter three, when it comes to the means of salvation, belief alone is mentioned. Also, the mention of water does not always include baptism. Baptism is not specifically named in the entire chapter, so this interpretation is not in-disputable. What is indisputable is that verses 15 and 16 teach that belief alone leads to eternal life.

d. 1 Corinthians 15:29 does not say that baptism for the dead was a Christian practice.

(1) Paul used baptism for the dead as an example for the resur-rection, not for Christian conduct.

(2) The fact that Paul used "they" (third person plural) throughout the verse suggests that he was not speaking of the Christians at Corinth or he would have used "you," nor was he speaking of himself or he would have used "I."

(3) He carefully separated the practice from Christianity with his choice of pronouns.[135]

(4) Evidently some were practicing baptism for the dead in the area, but Paul's reference to it is not an endorsement of the practice any more than his quotation of pagan poets is an en-dorsement of them (Acts 17:28; Titus 1:12).

e. Paul's exhortation in Philippians 2:12 to "work out your salvation with fear and trembling" is not the same as saying "earn your sal-vation through works."

(1) Paul was urging the Philippians not to give up on their Christian life, but to persevere to the end.

(2) Verse 13 puts an end to the question of works, saying it is not us but God who works through us to do good.

---

[135]Paul is arguing here for the resurrection, not baptism, and uses their point of view to do so. He is not building a case for baptizing the dead.

f. James's statement in 2:26, "faith without deeds is dead," must be understood in the context of this entire book, which teaches that genuine faith produces good works; that is, good deeds are the mark of true faith.

(1) Nowhere does James explicitly or implicitly state that human works contribute to salvation. The born again experience, mentioned in 1:18–21, comes through the "word of truth ... planted in you" (vv. 18, 21). Such language removes all possibility that human works can contribute to salvation.

(2) James (2:14–26) does not contradict Paul on justification, neither does James provide salvation through works, for faith always precedes works in his writings.

g. 1 Peter 3:19 says that Christ "went and preached to the spirits in prison," not that Christ went into hades and preached salvation to the dead. The key to understanding this verse is that the antecedent to the word "whom" (v. 19) is the Holy Spirit (v. 18). "Through whom" refers to the Holy Spirit: "He [Christ] was ... alive by the Spirit, through whom also he went and preached." Christ preached to those in the days of Noah "through" the Holy Spirit, while they were still living, not after they had died. Noah's message was Christ's message through the Holy Spirit, which is perfectly consistent with 1 Peter 1:11, "to which the Spirit of Christ in them was pointing when he predicted the sufferings of Christ and the glories that would follow."

h. 1 Peter 4:6 does not say that Jesus preached salvation to the dead.

(1) The context shows that the preaching occurred while these were alive, not after death.

(2) Chapter one clearly shows that Christ, in the Spirit, spoke through the Old Testament prophets, which is how those "in the days of Noah" (3:20) and all others were preached to (while they were alive).

D. *The Biblical Doctrine of Christ's Atonement and Salvation*

1. Scripture explicitly teaches the vicarious atonement of Jesus Christ for the sins of the world.

a. Jesus Christ is God come in human form to reconcile the world to himself (2 Cor. 5:18–19; Phil. 2:6–8).

(1) This is accomplished through the shed blood of Jesus (Rom. 5:10).

(2) Christ's atonement is substitutionary, done on behalf of sinners (Isa. 53:4–12; Matt. 20:28; 26:28; 1 John 2:1–2). Christ is the perfect sacrifice because he was sinless and therefore needed no cleansing himself (2 Cor. 5:21; Heb. 4:15; 7:26). He took upon himself the penalty for our sins (Gal. 3:13).

69

      (3) The atonement was accomplished upon the cross (not the garden of Gethsamane), where Christ bore our sins (1 Peter 2:24).

      (4) In Christ the entire work of atoning for sin was completed "once for all" (Heb. 7:27).

      (5) Through the atonement we are bought with a price (1 Cor. 6:20; 7:23).

  b. The atonement is appropriated through faith in Jesus Christ as Lord (Rom. 3:25; Heb. 9:14).

      (1) A person is saved by grace through faith (Eph. 2:8–10).

      (2) A person is not saved by his or her righteousness or works (Eph. 2:8; Titus 3:5).

      (3) Whoever believes in Jesus shall be saved (John 3:16; 20:31; Acts 16:31; Rom. 3:22; 10:9–10; 1 John 5:13).

2. Salvation is the work of God in regenerating sinners through the shed blood of Christ (Titus 3:5).

  a. Our sins are forgiven (1 John 1:9).

  b. We are justified (i.e., declared "not guilty" before God) through Christ (Rom. 3:24; 5:1).

  c. We are regenerated or born again (John 3:3; 2 Cor. 5:17; Eph. 2:8).

  d. We are sanctified, made holy, and set apart for God's use (1 Cor. 1:2; 1 Thess. 5:23).

3. Christians shall inherit heaven (Luke 10:20).

  a. Upon death we will dwell in the presence of God (Phil. 1:23; 2 Cor. 5:6).

  b. Jesus has prepared a place for his followers (John 14:2).

  c. It is one dwelling (not several levels) which is made by God (2 Cor. 5:1).

  d. We shall dwell there in eternal joy with Christ (Rev. 21:1–7).

IX. The Church

A. *The Mormon View of the Church Briefly Stated*

  1. The original church fell away from the truth after three centuries.

  2. The apostasy was universal and there was no true Christian church.

  3. Mormonism is the restoration of the original church.

  4. The true church is recognizable because it will have prophets, apostles and seventies (see Part I, section III.B. above).

  5. It will also have the proper authority, or priesthood, to act in Christ's name.

B. *Arguments Mormons Use to Support Their View of the Church*

  1. A restored church assumes an apostate church.

a. "Since the departure from the true gospel of Christ was to be universal, as the prophets foretold, and since such universal apostasy was confirmed in the statement of Jesus to Joseph Smith, it would follow that a restoration would be necessary."[136]

b. Since the entire church was apostate, no one on the earth had spiritual authority. "There was no one upon the earth holding the priesthood of God with authority to administer the ordinance of baptism unto them."[137]

c. The LDS Church is the only true church today. "The Church of Jesus Christ, as it was established in the days of the apostles, was governed by apostles, prophets, evangelists, high priests, seventies, and other officers, who are not found in the churches of the world today."[138]

2. General authorities govern the restored church (see Part I, section III.B above).

a. prophets (the first presidency)

b. apostles

c. seventies

d. presiding bishop

3. The authority of the restored church lies within the Aaronic and Melchizedekian priesthoods.

a. Distinctions between the two priesthoods: "Priesthood, without which the true church cannot exist, and without which the gospel cannot be administered, is always found among the Lord's people. The higher priesthood [i.e., Melchizedek] administers the whole gospel system; the lesser priesthood [i.e., Aaronic] can go no further than to operate the performances and ordinances of the law of Moses."[139]

b. The purpose of the Aaronic priesthood: "[The] Priesthood of Aaron holds authority to baptize by immersion for remission of sins."[140]

c. The purpose of the Melchizedekian priesthood: "Men holding the higher authority were sent to confer the Holy Ghost upon the converts in Samaria. Here appears the distinction between the authority of the lesser or Aaronic and the higher or Melchizedek Priesthood."[141]

---

[136]Richards, *A Marvelous Work and a Wonder*, 32.

[137]Richards, *A Marvelous Work and a Wonder*, 106.

[138]Joseph Fielding Smith, *Doctrines of Salvation*, 1:239.

[139]McConkie, *The Promised Messiah*, 410.

[140]Talmage, *Articles of Faith*, 135.

[141]Talmage, *Articles of Faith*, 168.

4. Mormons use Scripture (KJV) to support their view of the church.

a. Matthew 16:18—Jesus said he will build his church "upon this rock," referring to the rock of revelation (i.e., modern revelation).

b. Acts 20:30—When Paul predicted that "of your own selves shall men arise, speaking perverse things, to draw away disciples after them" (KJV), he was speaking about the church falling away.

c. 1 Corinthians 12:28—"God hath set some in the church, first apostles, secondarily prophets, thirdly teachers, after that miracles, then gifts of healings, helps, governments, diversities of tongues."

d. Ephesians 2:20—"And are built upon the foundation of the apostles and prophets, Jesus Christ himself being the chief cornerstone."

e. 2 Thessalonians 2:3—This verse predicts a universal apostasy from the true church.

f. 1 Timothy 4:1—Paul predicted that "in the latter times some shall depart from the faith, giving heed to seducing spirits, and doctrines of devils" (KJV), meaning an apostasy will occur.

C. *Refutation of Arguments Mormons Use to Support Their View of the Church*

1. The church of Jesus Christ, as outlined in the New Testament, would not fall away into apostasy.

a. If there is no apostasy there is no need for restoration.

(1) Jesus promised that the church would always remain: "the gates of Hades will not overcome it" (Matt. 16:18). To believe that the church fell away reveals a very weak view of Jesus; it is the same as saying he cannot withstand the enemies of his church.

(2) Jesus used two parables to teach that the church would endure—though some members would fall away. Jesus taught in the parable of the tares (Matt. 13:24–30) that the wheat (the church) was there all along—in the midst of the tares—and endured until the end. In the parable of the net of fish (Matt. 13:47–50) Jesus says that the angels will separate the wicked from the righteous, illustrating again that the church will remain. God allows weeds among wheat and bad fish among good, but the church will always remain.

(3) Paul also taught that the church would endure until the end (1 Cor. 1:8).

b. The verses in the New Testament that speak of a falling away do not make it all-inclusive; some will fall away, but nowhere does Scripture teach universal apostasy.

2. The Mormon notions of the priesthood and authority are unbiblical.

a. Jesus Christ is the only authority in the Christian church. Those who serve the church (apostles, prophets, teachers, etc.) all derive their authority from Christ (Matt. 28:18; Eph. 4:11).

b. The Aaronic (or Levitical) priesthood was only for those of the tribe of Levi (Num. 3:5–10).

  (1) The purpose of the Aaronic priesthood was fulfilled at the cross (Heb. 7:11–22; 10:8–18).

  (2) Jesus Christ replaced the temporary mediators (priests) as the true mediator (1 Tim. 2:5; Heb. 7:23–25).

c. The greater priesthood, the Melchizedekian priesthood, was held only by Melchizedek and Jesus (Heb. 7).

  (1) That Jesus was "another" (v. 11) priest after the order of Melchizedek shows that there were only two, Melchizedek and Jesus.

  (2) Jesus never vacated his position and still holds his Melchizedekian priesthood (v. 24). In verse 24, the Greek word *aparabatos*, translated "unchangeable" (KJV) or "permanent" (NIV), means that Jesus never passes his priesthood on to another. The J. B. Phillips translation correctly renders it "untransferable."

3. Mormons misinterpret Scripture to support their view of authority.

a. Matthew 16:18

  (1) The Mormon claim that the rock spoken of here is the rock of revelation is not consistent with the context of the passage.

  (2) The context is Jesus' question, "Who do you say I am?" (v. 15) and Peter's response, "You are the Christ, the Son of the living God" (v. 16).

  (3) Jesus' statement, "this rock," in verse 18 refers back to Peter's answer in verse 16: "You are the Christ, the Son of the living God." The rock that the church is built upon is Jesus Christ himself.[142]

b. Acts 20:30—This verse speaks of deceivers coming in to destroy the church, not that the entire church will become apostate.

c. 1 Corinthians 12:28—Paul here lists some of the gift-offices of the church.

  (1) These offices are part of a discussion on spiritual gifts in the context of chapter 12.

  (2) Paul does not say there are twelve with the gift of apostleship, or three with the gift of prophecy, but leaves such numbers wide open because many had the gifts—though verse 29

---

[142]There are Christian denominations that interpret "rock" differently, but none accept the Mormon position.

shows that not all had them. Paul does place apostles first and prophets second, while the Mormon church places prophets first and apostles second. Thus, whatever one thinks of Paul's teaching, the Mormons clearly have it wrong. In addition, the word for *apostle* is used of twenty-three individuals in the New Testament, eighteen of whom lived at the same time. The original twelve apostles were the foundation (Eph. 2:20) and the other apostles mentioned had a gift for spreading the church into new areas.

   d. Ephesians 2:20—This verse refers to the foundation of the church (apostles, prophets, and Jesus Christ) in the past tense. The church, present tense, is being built upon that foundation.

     (1) The foundation for such a church in progress cannot be replaced without destroying the structure.

     (2) Therefore, the foundation mentioned here is the original Twelve (with Judas replaced by Matthias, Acts 1:12–26).

   e. Ephesians 4:11

     (1) Paul here lists specific church offices of apostle, prophet, evangelist, pastor, and teacher, which are separated from the foundation by the fact that they are gifts.

     (2) Such gifts explain why the word apostle is used of so many people outside of the Twelve in the New Testament simultaneously.[143]

   f. 2 Thessalonians 2:3—While this verse does speak of some falling away, it does not predict that there will be total apostasy.

   g. 1 Timothy 4:1–2—Paul speaks of deceivers within the church, but such deceivers are noticeable precisely because the church still remains.

D. The Biblical Doctrine on the Church

  1. The Christian church is an earthly manifestation of the body of Jesus Christ.

   a. The name of the church is incidental; Scripture records several names to describe fellowships of believers.[144]

   b. There are many members but one body (1 Cor. 12:12–27).

  2. The church is under the Lordship of Christ, the head, who delegates authority to its members (Col. 1:18; 1 Cor. 12:28; Eph. 4:11–12).

---

[143]Those with the gift of apostleship outside of the Twelve were Barnabas (Acts 14:14), James (Gal. 1:19), Andronicus (Rom. 16:7), Junias (Rom. 16:7), and perhaps others (Timothy, Silas, and Apollos).

[144]A few biblical examples are: the church of God (Acts 20:28), the churches of Christ (Rom. 16:16), the church in Ephesus/Smyrna/Pergamum/Thyatira/Sardis/Philadelphia/Laodicea (Rev. 2 and 3), the church of the firstborn (Heb. 12:23), and the church of the living God (1 Tim. 3:15).

3. The New Testament describes individual church members by several terms.
   a. Christians (Acts 11:26)
   b. Disciples (Matt. 28:19)
   c. The family of believers (Gal. 6:10)
   d. Brothers (1 John 3:14)
   e. The elect (Matt. 24:22)
   f. Children of God (1 John 3:1)
   g. Saints (Rev. 5:8)
   h. Sheep (John 10:27)
   i. God's temple (1 Cor. 3:16; 6:19)
4. The church as a whole is known by several descriptions.
   a. Christ's body (1 Cor. 12:27)
   b. The bride of Christ (Rev. 21:9)
   c. A spiritual house (1 Peter 2:5)
   d. God's family (Eph. 3:15)
   e. God's household (1 Tim. 3:15)
   f. The pillar and foundation of the truth (1 Tim. 3:15)

X. The End Times

A. *The Mormon View of the End Times Briefly Stated*

1. There will be a gathering of Israel and great tribulation for the church.
2. Then Jesus Christ will personally and literally return to earth.
3. Christ will set up a millennial reign.
4. Christ will judge the living and the dead.
5. The righteous will be rewarded by receiving one of the three heavenly kingdoms.
6. The unrighteous will be punished in hell.
7. Those in hell can gain heaven if they repent and obey Christ.

B. *Mormon Arguments Used to Support Their View of the End Times*

1. There will be several gatherings of people—one of Jews, one of Ephraim, and one for the lost ten tribes—and great tribulation for the church.
   a. The tenth Article of Faith states: "We believe in the literal gathering of Israel and in the restoration of the Ten Tribes; that Zion (the New Jerusalem) will be built upon the American continent; that Christ will reign personally upon the earth; and, that the earth will be renewed and receive this paradisiacal glory."

      b. Apostle Talmage explains, "It is evident that the plan of gathering comprises: 1. Assembling in the land of Zion of the people of Israel from the nations of the earth. 2. Return of the Jews to Jerusalem. 3. Restoration of the Lost Tribes."[145]

      c. Prophet Ezra Taft Benson taught that "the Lord has warned and forewarned us against a day of great tribulation and given us counsel, through His servants, on how we can be prepared for these difficult times. Have we heeded His counsel?"[146]

2. Jesus Christ will return in his resurrected body. "The Lord's ascension was accomplished; it was as truly a literal departure of a material Being ... the same Being who ascended from Olivet in His immortalized body of flesh and bones, shall return, descending from the heavens, in similarly material form and substance."[147]

3. When Christ returns he will set up his millennial reign. "The resurrection of the just will come with the return of our Lord and the commencement of his millennial reign."[148]

4. After Christ judges the living and the dead, the righteous will enter into one of three degrees of heaven (see section VIII.B.5. above).

5. The unrighteous will be sent to hell.

      a. Those who fight against the Mormon church and those who murder will go to hell.

          (1) Those who fight against Mormonism are the sons of perdition. "The sons of perdition—those evil and defiant rebels who, having a perfect knowledge that Jesus is the Lord, yet fight against God and Christ and the holy gospel [the Mormon gospel]—having been resurrected, will yet remain as though there had been no redemption made."[149]

          (2) Few people are sons of perdition. "The comparative few who reach this state of extreme degradation are doomed to dwell 'with the devil and his angels in eternity, where their worm dieth not, and the fire is not quenched, which is their torment.'"[150]

      b. Those in hell still have opportunity to repent and can atone for their sins. "The wicked and ungodly will suffer the vengeance of eternal fire in hell until they finally obey Christ, repent of their sins, and gain forgiveness therefrom. Then they shall obtain the

---

[145]Talmage, *Articles of Faith,* 337.

[146]Benson, *Teachings of the Prophet Ezra Taft Benson,* 706.

[147]Talmage, *Jesus the Christ,* 679.

[148]McConkie, *Mormon Doctrine,* 493.

[149]McConkie, *A New Witness for the Articles of Faith,* 120.

[150]James Talmage, *Vitality of Mormonism* (Boston: Richard G. Badger, 1919), 288.

resurrection and an inheritance in the telestial and not the celestial kingdom."[151]

6. Mormons use Scripture to support their view of the end times.

  a. John 14:2—The many "mansions" (KJV) that Jesus went to prepare for us are the various degrees of heaven.

  b. 1 Corinthians 15:40–42—This passage shows the degrees of heaven: "There are also celestial bodies, and bodies terrestrial; but the glory of the celestial is one, and the glory of the terrestrial is another. There is one glory of the sun, and another glory of the moon, and another glory of the stars: for one star differeth from another star in glory."

  c. 2 Corinthians 12:2—The "third heaven" represents the celestial kingdom.

C. Refutation of Mormon Arguments on the End Times

1. The tribes were not lost.

  a. The house of Israel was represented in Jerusalem at the time of the crucifixion (Acts 2:22, 36).

    (1) When Peter addressed the "men of Israel" (verse 22), he was saying that the "house of Israel" (verse 36) was represented.

    (2) Every living member of every tribe does not need to be present in order for the house of Israel to be represented.

  b. James addressed his epistle to "the twelve tribes scattered among the nations" (1:1), which indicates they were present and known, even though they were scattered.

2. Mormons misinterpret Scripture to prove their view of the end times.

  a. John 14:2—When Jesus promised to go to the Father and prepare a place for us, he did not hint at the idea of three heavenly kingdoms, but portrayed only one kingdom within heaven.

  b. 1 Corinthians 15:40–42—This passage does not teach that there are three kingdoms in heaven, but rather shows several glories within the one kingdom of heaven. Celestial and terrestrial are mentioned as contrasts between the glory of heaven and earth. The absence of the telestial is troubling to Mormons.

  c. 2 Corinthians 12:2—Even though Paul used "the third heaven" as a description of paradise (v. 4), it by no means represents one of the Mormon kingdoms. The Jews divided heaven into the atmosphere, the stars, and the dwelling place of God.[152]

D. The Biblical Doctrine of the End Times

1. Jesus Christ will return physically for his church.

---

[151]McConkie, *Mormon Doctrine*, 816.

[152]Barnes, *Barnes' Notes on the New Testament*, 902.

a. Jesus will return physically from heaven (Matt. 24:30; 26:64).

b. It will be in the same way he ascended (Acts 1:9–11).

c. No one knows when Jesus will return (Matt. 24:42–44; Mark 13:32–36; Luke 12:35–40).

2. Jesus Christ will judge the nations and individuals.

a. He will judge individuals and the nations (Matt. 12:36; 25:32).

b. He will judge Israel (Isa. 1:24–26).

c. He will judge believers and unbelievers (Matt. 25:31–46).

d. He will judge Satan and his angels (Rev. 20:10; Jude 5–6).

3. Those who put their faith in Jesus during their life on earth will enjoy everlasting life with him (John 3:16; Matt. 25:34; Rev. 21:1–7, 21–27).

4. Those who reject Jesus as the only way of salvation will go to hell (Matt. 25:41, 46; Rev. 20:11–15).

Part III: Witnessing Tips

I. The Mormon Frame of Reference

A. The Apostasy of Non-Mormon Christians

1. Mormons believe that non-LDS Christians are actually apostates, since Mormonism is the only true organization or church.

2. Mormons believe non-LDS Christians have fallen away from the truth with no hope of gaining personal salvation outside of Mormonism.

3. Mormonism is the only cult that specifically states in its scripture that Christian denominations are false. "The Presbyterians were most decided against the Baptists and Methodists, and used all the powers of reason and sophistry to prove their errors, or at least, to make people think they were in error. On the other hand, the Baptists and Methodists in their turn were equally zealous in endeavoring to establish their own tenets and disprove all others. In the midst of this war of words and tumult of opinions, I often said to myself: What is to be done? Who of all these parties are right; or, are they all wrong together? If any one of them be right, which is it, and how shall I know it?... I asked the Personages who stood above me in the light, which of all the sects was right (for at that time it had never entered into my heart that all were wrong).... I was answered that I must join none of them, for they were all wrong ... all their creeds were an abomination ... all those professors were all corrupt."[153]

4. The Book of Mormon recognizes two churches: "the church of the Lamb of God" and "the church of the devil" (1 Nephi 14:10); Mormons believe they are the only church of God and all other churches are of the devil.

B. Christians Have No Authority from God

1. The terms *authority* and *priesthood* are interchangeable and almost synonymous to Mormons.

2. Unless one has the Mormon priesthood there is no authority to act in the name of Christ.

3. Mormon temple garments represent this authority, which reminds the Mormon of his temple covenants and priesthood authority (see Part I, section II.E.4 above). Therefore, those who do not have such garments are viewed by Mormons as devoid of authority.

---

[153]Joseph Smith, Pearl of Great Price, Joseph Smith–History 1:9–19.

4. Mormon missionaries will often say, "We are here to teach and not be taught." Mormon missionaries are addressed as "Elder" and "Sister," even by those who are not members of their church, thus granting them authority in the eyes of those with whom they are speaking.

C. *Persecution and Mormon Identity*

1. Mormons regularly rehearse at church meetings their history of persecution to remind them of their past.

2. Mormons believe they are "the persecuted Church."

3. Any opposition is viewed as persecution, and opposing literature is often called "Anti-Mormon."

4. The "Anti-Mormon" label releases Mormons from feeling obligated to respond to the challenges of such literature on the basis that it is persecution.

D. *The Mormon Testimony*

1. Mormons are encouraged to bear their testimony weekly. A Mormon testimony is a memorized statement of belief.

2. The testimony in essence is, "I testify that Joseph Smith was a prophet of God and died a martyr for the faith, that the Book of Mormon is true, that the Church of Jesus Christ of Latter-day Saints is the only true restored church, and that there is a living prophet upon the earth today."

3. Mormons frequently speak of "gaining" and "losing" a testimony.

   a. Gaining a testimony

      (1) Those who gain a testimony speak of a burning feeling or sensation in their bosom.

      (2) This feeling is understood to be the influence of the Holy Spirit testifying to the truthfulness of the testimony.

   b. Losing a testimony

      (1) Mormons who have lost their testimony no longer have the feeling that accompanies it.

      (2) This indicates that they have some sin blocking the influence of the Holy Spirit.

   c. Since those outside Mormonism obviously have no testimony, Mormons encourage them to pray for a testimony of Mormonism.

E. *Grace Vs. Works*

1. In the Mormon frame of reference, God's grace, as spoken of in Christianity, is a vague application of belief accompanied by a false hope of assurance which encourages Christians to live licentiously and break the ten commandments at will.

   a. Mormons call Christian preachers "gracers" because they preach "salvation by grace."

    b. A person who is saved by grace alone and not by works also is viewed as having license to sin.

  2. Mormons repudiate Christian preaching of salvation by grace and not by works, since Christ's mission was to be our "exemplar" (i.e., example) and to help us work toward human perfection (i.e., to earn our salvation).

II. Countering the Mormon Frame of Reference

A. Apostasy and the True Church

  1. Show Mormons that the verses on apostasy in the Bible deny a universal and total apostasy.

  2. The Bible teaches that *some* will fall away from the truth, but that a remnant of true believers will always be present on the earth.

    a. Matthew 16:18

      (1) Point out the contrast between the Jesus of Matthew's Gospel, who said his church will not fail, and the Jesus of Joseph Smith's writing, who claimed the church was apostate.

      (2) This is no small contrast because the two statements are irreconcilable.

      (3) Mormons must choose which "Jesus" is telling the truth: the Jesus of Matthew or the Jesus of Joseph Smith.

    b. 2 Corinthians 11:4—Paul warned believers about those who preach "a Jesus other than the Jesus" of Scripture.

  3. Confess your faith in the Jesus of Matthew, Paul, and the other New Testament writers—any other Jesus is false.

  4. The true Christian church is one body, serving one Lord, through one faith (Eph. 4:4–5).

    a. The genuine faith of Christianity spans all denominational barriers.

      (1) We agree on the essentials of the faith (Eph. 4:1–6).

      (2) We allow for differences on the nonessentials (Rom. 14:1–22).

    b. We are many members but one body (1 Cor. 12:14–20).

B. The Source of Authority for Christians

  1. The Christian's authority does not come from the laying on of hands; it comes directly through God indwelling us (1 Cor. 6:19).

  2. Jesus has all authority or power in heaven and earth; the Greek word *exousia* is translated as "authority" or "power" in Matthew 28:18.

    a. The same Greek word is used of the Christian believer in John 1:12.

    b. Jesus Christ has given us authority through believing in his name.

  3. Through faith in Christ we are made new (2 Cor. 5:17).

a. As new creations in him (Eph. 4:24) we receive his authority (John 1:12).

b. Through faith in Christ we become part of the holy priesthood of believers (1 Peter 2:5–9).

4. Therefore, our authority is not our own but is derived from Christ; we serve by the authority of Christ, who dwells in us by faith.

C. Anti-Mormon Sentiment and Behavior

1. Truth can stand on its own merits; making derogatory remarks about a group of people or their literature is no way to discuss matters of truth.

2. The fact that the Mormon Church has been persecuted is nothing to rejoice in.

   a. Persecution cannot be an indication that a group possesses ultimate truth because most Christian denominations have endured some amount of persecution.

   b. Furthermore, cults with which both Mormons and Christians disagree also have endured persecution (e.g., Jehovah's Witness, Baha'ism, and the Unification Church).

D. The Christian Testimony

1. Always share your testimony with Mormons. Tell them how God saved you through the sacrifice of his Son.

2. Note the contrast between the Mormon testimony, which has no personal encounters with Christ, and the Christian testimony, which tells of Christ's saving power in the lives of sinners.

3. If a Mormon bears his testimony, then ask him to kindly listen to yours.

E. Grace and Not Works

1. Early in your conversation with Mormons stress the point that salvation by grace is not a license to sin.

   a. Discuss Romans 6:1–4, how we who profess faith in Christ have died to sin.

   b. The Bible condemns those who use the gospel to excuse their sin, and we should, too.

2. When witnessing to Mormons point out that the very act of witnessing is a "work" that follows your salvation. We do good works because we are saved, we do not do good works in order to be saved (Eph. 2:8–10).

III. Suggestions for Witnessing to Mormons

A. Bible Translations

1. Because Mormons use the King James Version of Scripture (or the New King James Version), you may increase your chances of gaining an ear if you also use this version.

2. Sometimes it is difficult for Mormons to accept other new translations of the Bible, so be ready to explain why your translation is accurate.

B. Interpretation

1. Sometimes Mormons may say, "that's just your interpretation." This may just be an attempt to deflect a good point made by the Christian.

2. Ask Mormons to examine the text word-for-word with you, while you show why the context supports your understanding.

3. The correct interpretation will agree with the history, grammar, and context.[154]

C. Terminology

1. Define your terms early in your conversation and take notes on points made or side issues to which you may wish to return.

2. Agreed-upon definitions of terms prevents equivocation later in the conversation.

3. When necessary, return to your stated definitions so that distortions may be clarified.

4. When you are discussing an important subject and a valid secondary issue surfaces, take a note of it instead of losing your place in a more important topic.

D. Scripture References

Remember that one well-explained verse is more helpful than ten off-handed verses.

IV. Common Mistakes Christians Make When Witnessing to Mormons

A. Prayer

1. Prayer for the Holy Spirit's guidance is fundamental to effective witnessing to Mormons (or any non-Christian group).

2. Those who rely on human wisdom instead of God's underestimate the power of sin and Satan to obscure the truth.

---

[154]A number of good articles and books may be consulted on proper biblical interpretation. See Douglas Stewart and Gordon D. Fee, *How to Read the Bible for All It's Worth* (Grand Rapids: Zondervan, 1982).

3. We are not witnessing for ourselves, so we must have the guidance of the Lord in the forefront.

B. Focus

1. There is a place for bringing in Mormon history, false prophecies, and obscure doctrines, but don't make these the sole purpose for meeting with Mormons. The goal in witnessing to Mormons is to proclaim the message of the saving grace of Jesus.

2. There have been many Mormons who on their own, or with the aid of dissenters, have left Mormonism without following Jesus as Lord, but the one is just as unsaved as the other, so don't lose sight of the focus.

3. We are to plant the "seed" of the Word of God (Mark 4).

C. Integrity

1. Mormons are people for whom Christ died; witnessing is not a means of venting anger or exalting knowledge or winning an argument.

2. It is possible to win the argument but lose the soul.

3. Don't prove a point at the expense of proclaiming salvation.

Part IV:
Selected Bibliography

I. Primary Sources

A. Newspapers

Deseret News, Salt Lake City, Utah

Deseret News, Church News Section, Salt Lake City, Utah

The Salt Lake Tribune, Salt Lake City, Utah

B. Periodicals

Brigham Young University Studies, Provo, Utah

Dialogue: A Journal of Mormon Thought, Arlington, Virginia

The Ensign, Salt Lake City, Utah

Sunstone, Salt Lake City, Utah

Utah Historical Quarterly, Salt Lake City, Utah

Utah Holiday Magazine, Salt Lake City, Utah

C. Books

Allen, James B., and Glen M. Leonard. *The Story of the Latter-day Saints*. Salt Lake City: Deseret Book Co., 1976, 1993.

Arrington, Leonard J., and Davis Bitton. *The Mormon Experience*. New York: Random House, 1980.

Backman, Milton V. *Joseph Smith's First Vision*. Salt Lake City: Bookcraft, 1971.

Brodie, Fawn M. *No Man Knows My History—The Life of Joseph Smith*. New York: Knoft, 1957.

Brooks, Juanita. *The Mountain Meadows Massacre*. Stanford: Stanford University Press, 1950.

Heinerman, John, and Anson Shupe. *The Mormon Corporate Empire*. Boston: Beacon, 1985.

Howard, Richard P. *Restoration Scriptures—A Study of Their Textual Development*. Independence, Mo.: Herald, 1969.

Hunter, Milton R. *Gospel Through the Ages*. Salt Lake City: Deseret Book Co., 1958.

Ludlow, Daniel H., ed. *Encyclopedia of Mormonism*. 5 vols. New York: Macmillan, 1992.

McConkie, Bruce R. *Mormon Doctrine*. Salt Lake City: Bookcraft, 1966.

Richards, F. D., comp. *Journal of Discourses*. 26 vols. Liverpool: Latter-day Saint Book Depot, 1855–1886.

Richards, LeGrand. *A Marvelous Work and a Wonder*. Salt Lake City: Deseret Book Co., 1976.

Roberts, B. H. *A Comprehensive History of the Church of Jesus Christ of Latter-day Saints*. 6 vols. Salt Lake City: Deseret Book Co., 1930.

Smith, Joseph Jr. The Book of Mormon. Palmyra, N.Y.: Grandin, 1830; Rev. ed., Salt Lake City: Corporation of the Church of Jesus Christ of Latter-day Saints, 1981.

————. The Doctrine and Covenants. Kirtland, Ohio: 1835; Rev. ed., Salt Lake City: Corporation of the Church of Jesus Christ of Latter-day Saints, 1981.

————. *Documented History of the Church of Jesus Christ of Latter-day Saints*. 6 vols. edited by B. H. Roberts. Salt Lake City: Deseret Book Co., 1978.

————. Pearl of Great Price. Liverpool: 1851; Rev. ed., Salt Lake City: Corporation of the Church of Jesus Christ of Latter-day Saints, 1981.

Smith, Joseph Fielding. *Answers to Gospel Questions*. 3 vols. Salt Lake City: Deseret Book Co., 1957.

————. *Doctrines of Salvation*. 3 vols. Salt Lake City: Bookcraft, 1959.

————, comp. *Teachings of the Prophet Joseph Smith*. Salt Lake City: Deseret Book Co., 1949.

Talmage, James E. *Articles of Faith*. Salt Lake City: Deseret Book Co., 1981.

Widtsoe, John A., comp. *Discourses of Brigham Young*. Salt Lake City: Deseret Book Co., 1976.

II. Secondary Sources

Cowan, Marvin. *Mormon Claims Answered*. Salt Lake City: Cowan Publications, 1975.

Fraser, Gordon H. *Is Mormonism Christian?* Chicago: Moody Press, 1977.

Geer, Thelma. *Mormonism, Mama and Me!* Chicago: Moody Press, 1986.

Hoekema, Anthony A. *The Four Major Cults*. Grand Rapids: Eerdmans, 1963.

Hunt, Dave, and Ed Decker. *The God-Makers*. Eugene, Oreg.: Harvest House, 1982.

Larson, Charles M. *By His Own Hand upon Papyrus*. Grand Rapids: Institute for Religious Research, 1992.

McElveen, Floyd C. *The Mormon Illusion*. Ventura, Calif.: Regal Books, 1976.

McKeever, Bill. *Answering Mormons' Questions*. Minneapolis: Bethany House, 1991.

Martin, Walter R. *The Maze of Mormonism*. Ventura, Calif.: Gospel Light, 1978.

———. *The Kingdom of the Cults*. 5th ed. Minneapolis: Bethany House, 1985.

Scott, Latayne C. *Why We Left Mormonism*. Grand Rapids: Baker, 1990.

Tanner, Jerald, and Sandra Tanner. *The Changing World of Mormonism*. Chicago: Moody Press, 1980.

———. *Mormonism—Shadow or Reality?* 5th ed. Salt Lake City: Utah Lighthouse Ministry, 1985.

Part V:
Parallel Comparison Chart

Mormonism	The Bible
Continued Revelation	

"The canon of scripture is not full. God has never revealed at any time that he would cease to speak forever to men" (*Gospel Doctrine*, 36).

"Modern revelation is necessary. . . . If we are permitted to believe that he has spoken, we must and do believe that he continues to speak, because he is unchangeable" (*Gospel Doctrine*, 36).

"From Jerusalem all the way around to Illyricum, I *have fully proclaimed the gospel* of Christ" (Rom. 15:19).

"I felt I had to write and urge you to contend for *the faith that was once for all entrusted* to the saints" (Jude 3).

| **The Creator** | |

"The Gods organized and formed the heavens and earth. ...And they (the Gods) said: Let there be light; and there was light. And they (the Gods) comprehended the light. ...And the Gods called the light Day" (Pearl of Great Price, Book of Abraham, 4:1–5).

"In the beginning the head of the Gods called a council of the Gods; and they came together and concocted a plan to create and populate the world and people it" (*Journal of Discourses*, 6:5).

"In the beginning God created the heavens and the earth" (Gen. 1:1).

"You alone are the LORD. You made the heavens, even the highest heavens, and all their starry host, the earth and all that is on it, the seas and all that is in them. You give life to everything, and the multitudes of heaven worship you" (Neh. 9:6).

The Uniqueness of God

"I will preach on the plurality of Gods. . . . I wish to declare I have always and in all congregations, when I have preached on the subject of Deity, it has been the plurality of Gods" (*Documentary History of the Church*, 6:474).

"We have imagined and supposed that God was God from all eternity. I will refute that idea, and take away the veil, so that you can see" (*Documentary History of the Church*, 6:304).

"Hear, O Israel: The LORD our God, the LORD is one" (Deut. 6:4).

"Before me no god was formed, nor will there be one after me" (Isa. 43:10).

"Apart from me there is no God" (Isa. 44:6).

The Trinity

"Many men say there is one God; the Father, the Son, and the Holy Ghost are only one God! I say that this is a strange God anyhow—three in one, and one in three!... He would be a wonderfully big God—He would be a giant or a monster" (*Documentary History of the Church*, 6:476).

"This revealed doctrine of the composition and nature of the Godhead teaches that there are at least three Gods" (*Evidences and Reconciliation*, 65).

"Hear, O Israel: The LORD our God, the LORD is one" (Deut. 6:4).

"Go and make disciples of all nations, baptizing them in the name of the Father and of the Son and of the Holy Spirit" (Matt. 28:19).

"There are different kinds of gifts but *the same Spirit*. There are different kinds of service, but *the same Lord*. There are different kinds of worship, but *the same God*" (1 Cor. 12:4–6, emphasis added).

The Nature of God the Father

"First, God himself, who sits enthroned in yonder heavens, is a man like unto one of yourselves" (*Times and Seasons*, 5:613).

"The Father has a body of flesh and bones as tangible as man's" (Doctrine and Covenants, 130:22).

"For I am God, and not man—the Holy One among you" (Hos. 11:9).

"God is spirit" (John 4:24).

"A spirit hath not flesh and bones" (Luke 24:39 KJV).

The Virgin Birth of Jesus Christ

"When the virgin Mary conceived the child Jesus, the Father had begotten him in his own likeness. He was not begotten by the Holy Ghost. ...Now remember from this time forth, and forever, that Jesus Christ was not begotten by the Holy Ghost" (*Journal of Discourses*, 1:50–51).

"The body in which He performed His mission in the flesh was sired by that same Holy Being we worship as God, our Eternal Father" (*Teachings of the Prophet Ezra Taft Benson*, 7).

"She [Mary] was found to be with child through the Holy Spirit" (Matt. 1:18).

"'How will this be,' Mary asked the angel, 'since I am a virgin?'" (Luke 1:34).

"The Holy Spirit will come upon you [Mary], and the power of the Most High will overshadow you" (Luke 1:35).

The Atonement of Jesus Christ

"It is true that the blood of the Son of God was shed for sins through the fall and those committed by men, yet men can commit sins which it can never remit" (*Journal of Discourses*, 4:59).

"Joseph Smith taught that there were certain sins so grievous that man may commit, that they will place the transgressors beyond the power of the atonement of Christ" (*Doctrines of Salvation*, 1:138).

"The blood of Christ will never wipe that out, your own blood must atone for it" (*Journal of Discourses*, 3:247).

"If we walk in the light, as he is in the light, we have fellowship with one another, and the blood of Jesus, his Son, purifies us from all sin" (1 John 1:7).

"To him who loves us and has freed us from our sins by his blood" (Rev. 1:5).

"So Christ was sacrificed once to take away the sins of many people" (Heb. 9:28).

The Holy Spirit

"The Holy Ghost is the third member of the Godhead. He is a Personage of Spirit, a Spirit Person, a *Spirit Man*, a Spirit Entity. He can be in only one place at one time and he does not and cannot transform himself into any other form or image than that of the *Man whom he is*" (*Mormon Doctrine*, 358 [emphasis added]).

"You have lied to the Holy Spirit. ...You have not lied to men but to God" (Acts 5:3–4).

"Where can I go from your Spirit? Where can I flee from your presence? If I go up to the heavens, you are there; if I make my bed in the depths, you are there" (Ps. 139: 7–8).

Human Nature

"You have got to learn how to be gods yourselves, and to be kings and priests to God, the same as all gods have done before you" (*Documentary History of the Church*, 6:306).

"Then shall they be gods, because they have no end. . . . Then shall they be gods. . . . Abraham . . . Isaac . . . and Jacob . . . are not angels but are gods" (Doctrine and Covenants, 132:20, 37).

"Moses replied, 'It will be as you say, so that you may know there is no one like the Lord our God'" (Ex. 8:10).

"How great you are, O Sovereign LORD! There is no one like you, and there is no God but you" (2 Sam. 7:22).

"I am God, and not man—the Holy One among you" (Hosea 11:9).

Sin

"Divine justice forbids that we be accounted sinners solely because our parents transgressed" (Talmage, *Articles of Faith*, 475).

"We believe that men will be punished for their own sins, and not for Adam's transgression" (Articles of Faith, 2).

"Therefore, just as sin entered the world through man [Adam], and death through sin, and in this way death came to all men, because all sinned" (Rom. 5:12).

"Through the disobedience of the one man [Adam] the many were made sinners" (Rom. 5:19).

Salvation

"Full salvation is attained by virtue of knowledge, truth, righteousness, and all true principles. Many conditions must exist in order to make such salvation available to men. Without continuous revelation, the ministering of angels, the working of miracles, the prevalence of gifts of the spirit, there would be no salvation. There is no salvation outside the Church of Jesus Christ of Latter-day Saints" (*Mormon Doctrine*, 670).

"It is by grace you have been saved, through faith—and this not from yourselves, it is the gift of God—not by works, so that no one can boast" (Eph. 2:8–9).

"He saved us, not because of righteous things we had done, but because of his mercy" (Titus 3:5).

Eternal Retribution

"Those who live lives of wickedness may also be heirs of salvation, that is, they too shall be redeemed from death and from hell eventually. These, however, must suffer in hell the torments of the damned until they pay the price of their sinning, for the blood of Christ will not cleanse them" (*Doctrines of Salvation*, 2:133–34).

"Then they [those who do not follow Christ] will go away to eternal punishment" (Matt. 25:46).

"It is better for you to enter life maimed than with two hands to go into hell, where the fire never goes out" (Mark 9:43).